RHYME reading &WRITING

Edited by Roger Beard

Hodder & Stoughton

A MEMBER OF THE HODDER HEADLINE GROUP

Order queries: please contact Bookpoint Ltd, 39 Milton Park, Abingdon, Oxon
OX14 4TD. Telephone: (44) 01235 400414, Fax: (44) 1235 400454.
Lines are open from 9.00-6.00, Monday to Saturday, with a 24 hour message
answering service. Email address: orders@bookpoint.co.uk

British Library Cataloguing in Publication Data
A catalogue record for this title is available from The British Library

ISBN 0 340 62731 X

First published 1995
Impression number   12 11 10 9 8 7 6 5 4 3 2
Year   2004 2003 2002 2001 2000 1999 1998

Typeset by Transet Limited, Coventry, England.
Printed in Great Britain for Hodder & Stoughton Educational,
a division of Hodder Headline Plc, 338 Euston Road, London NW1 3BH
by Athenæum Press Ltd, Gateshead, Tyne & Wear.

CONTENTS

NOTES ABOUT THE CONTRIBUTORS

Tom McArthur has for the last ten years been an independent writer, editor, lecturer, consultant and broadcaster. Prior to this, he held various English teaching posts both in this country and abroad. He is Editor of *The Oxford Companion to the English Language* (1992) and of the quarterly journal *English Today: The International Review of the English Language* (CUP, founded 1984). He has had twenty books published, including *A Foundation Course for Language Teachers* (Cambridge, 1993) and *The Written Word: A Course in Controlled Composition* (Oxford, 1984).

Marian Whitehead is a Senior Lecturer in Education at Goldsmiths' College, University of London, and previously taught in infant and primary schools. She has researched and published extensively on language development and early childhood education and is the author of *Language and Literacy in the Early Years* (Paul Chapman, 1990). She is also a founder member of the Early Years Curriculum Group. Her main teaching responsibilities are for MA work in both language and literature in education and early childhood education. Her current research is part of a funded research project investigating notions of 'quality' and the early years curriculum in England and Wales. Her most recent paper (1994) outlines the possibilities for a narrative analysis of the emerging data (*Early Years*, 15, 1).

Usha Goswami is a lecturer in Experimental Psychology at the University of Cambridge, and a Fellow of St John's College, Cambridge. Her research focuses on reading and spelling development in young children and the role of analogies in children's learning. She has written two books: *Phonological Skills and Learning to Read* (Erlbaum, 1990) with Peter Bryant, and *Analogical Reasoning in Children* (Erlbaum, 1992). She was a recent winner of the British Psychology Society Spearman Medal for outstanding early career promise and has been a consultant to the National Curriculum Council on the teaching of English.

Sandy Brownjohn is well known for her books on teaching children to write poetry and has spoken on the subject throughout this country and abroad. Her books feature on many teacher education reading lists and she is much sought after to run courses in schools, teachers' centres, colleges and universities. In 1991, after twenty years as a full-time classroom teacher, followed by a period as an advisory teacher for English, she became a freelance writer and educational consultant, specialising in in-service training for teachers in schools. In addition to producing her books, Sandy also writes for BBC Radio and regularly reviews for the TES.

Brian Morse is a freelance children's author, poet, short story writer and novelist who has worked in primary education for twenty years. He has had fifteen books published, including two books of poems, *Picnic On the Moon* (Turton & Chambers/ Macmillan Pan Piper) and *Plenty Of Time* (Bodley Head/Red Fox). His Thimble Press publication *Poetry Books For Children*, covers more than two hundred titles for preschool ages up to the mid-teens and includes practical advice on ways to approach poetry in the classroom. Brian has run poetry workshops in many primary schools and also leads workshops for adults writing for children.

Frances James is currently an Advisory Headteacher (Learning Support) in the Northern Area of Suffolk, with a responsibility for a team of fifteen advisory and learning support teachers. She has taught in a first school and in an area support centre, been teacher-in-charge of a unit for children with emotional and behavioural difficulties and a senior teacher in a school for children with physical difficulties.

Georgina Boyes is a folklorist who has researched and lectured in cultural traditions at universities in Britain, Europe and North America. The author of over fifty academic works, she has also written extensively for radio, including 'A Proper Limitation' about Victorian women folklorists for Radio 4, and a six-part series on folksong, 'Voices from Arcadia', for Radio 2.

Her book *The Imagined Village* won the 1993 Katharine Briggs Folklore Award and got four stars in *Q*. She is an Honorary Research Associate at the Centre for English Cultural Tradition at Sheffield University and a consultant on English traditions to the World Arts Festival, Brooklyn, USA.

1

§§

INTRODUCTION

Roger Beard

> *I'll give you a piece of milk*
> *And a jug full of silk*

RHYME AND REPETITION

From an early age, children make up rhymes such as this.[1]
Children enjoy playing with words, particularly the kind of
play which involves *repetition*. Children like to repeat sounds,
words and phrases, savouring them by sound; children like
experimenting with words in the same way as they like trying
out new toys. Repeating words helps to keep them available for
inspection and allows indulgence in their distinctive features.
Repetition lies at the heart of much word play: in rhyme and
'near-rhymes' and in alliteration.

It has long been suggested that rhyme has a special place in the
development of children's language and literacy: nursery rhymes
have traditionally provided a distinctive way of encouraging
children to attend to the sounds and rhythms of the language;
attending to the sounds in words is an important part of
learning to read.

This book provides an exploration of rhyme, its relationships
with near-rhymes and alliteration and the related links with
reading and writing. It does so by bringing together a number
of distinguished teachers, writers and researchers who consider
rhyme from linguistic, literary and psychological perspectives.
The book will be of particular interest to teachers and parents
and to anyone who works with children in the pre-school and
primary school age ranges.

Earlier publications on this topic have sometimes been a little ambivalent about the educational significance of rhyme and a number of issues have been raised. While there has often been a general recognition of the value of children learning nursery rhymes, there have been frequently expressed fears of a decline in children's knowledge of them. There have also been uncertainties about the significance of children's preoccupation with nonsense in playing with words and about how this fits in with language development as a whole. There have been several other matters of debate: for example, how far children should be encouraged to tackle rhyme in their poetic writing; how far rhyme should be used in poetry which is written for children; and how far the 'stability' of rhymes might be exploited in helping children with special needs in learning to read and write. These issues can be placed against other questions about the rhymes and jingles which are common among today's children, whose visual experiences may be more sophisticated than those of their predecessors, but whose aural experiences may seem to be more limited. It is also important to establish some basic information about how rhyme and other word play can be used in English and an understanding of the technical terms which are used to refer to it. Such issues run through this book.

TERMS OF REFERENCE

In order to discuss these issues, a small number of technical terms need to be used and it may help to define these at this point. The terms 'rhyme' and 'alliteration' are generally well known. In the technical sense, *rhyme* refers to an identity of sound in two or more words which extends from the last stressed vowels to the ends of the words (e.g. 'm<u>ilk</u>' and s<u>ilk</u>'). This is sometimes referred to as 'end rhyme'. *Alliteration* refers to initial consonant sounds being repeated (e.g. 'silk' and '<u>s</u>un'). This feature is also sometimes called 'head-rhyme'.

Perhaps less well known are the various kinds of 'near-rhymes', including assonance and consonance and homeoteleuton. In *assonance* vowel sounds (on stressed syllables) are repeated (e.g. 'c<u>oa</u>t' and 'm<u>oa</u>n'). In *consonance* there is repetition of consonants in the same position in a sequence of words and after different vowels (e.g. 'spe<u>ck</u>' and 'flo<u>ck</u>'). Rhythm adds to such word play by providing flow and beat in word sequences. All these terms are further discussed and illustrated in subsequent chapters.

A RE-AWAKENED INTEREST

There seems to have been a recurrent concern that rhyme offers something special to children and yet that children's knowledge of traditional rhymes and jingles might not be as good as that of children in earlier generations. As long ago as 1853, James Orchard Halliwell wrote in his *The Nursery Rhymes of England* of the existence of an 'undying love for the popular remnants of the ancient Scandinavian nursery literature' and expressed relief that 'the infants and children of the nineteenth century have not, then, deserted the rhymes chanted so many ages since'.[2] A hundred years later, similar sentiments were expressed in the Bullock Report, from a Committee of Inquiry set up by the British government, which was concerned with the teaching of reading and other uses of English. The Report drew attention to how the use of rhymes, jingles and alliteration was helpful in focusing attention on the contrastive elements in words, while avoiding the distortions of analysing the sounds in words letter by letter. The Report expressed regret that the use of rhymes and other word play for this purpose had 'unaccountably fallen out of fashion'.[3] The Report did not provide evidence of this alleged decline in the use of rhymes, but if the conclusion was valid, then recent years have seen at least a restoration of interest in this topic. Prompted by research at the Universities of Oxford and Cambridge in particular[4], the educational significance of rhyme has been more widely appreciated and this in turn may be leading to greater exploitation of word play in schools, homes and communities.

THE SENSE IN NONSENSE

Kornei Chukovsky's *From Two to Five* is one of the most celebrated books about young children's word play, including the kind of 'nonsense verse' which appears at the beginning of this chapter. Chukovsky reports how a little girl aged four would sing 'I'll give you a piece of milk and a jug full of silk' for hours, annoying her grandmother, who would correct her every time.[5] His writing on this aspect of language development sometimes brought opposition. Children, he was told, need socially useful information, not the distortion of realistic facts.[6] The role of word play in language development, including the creation of 'topsy-turvey' rhyming games, is of great interest to all who work with and care for young children and is discussed in detail by Marian Whitehead in Chapter 3.

RHYME IN EARLY READING

The renewed interest in the significance of rhyme in literacy studies has been particularly inspired by research which has focused on early development in reading and spelling. As indicated in the reference to the Bullock Report above, the role of rhyme in early reading development has attracted attention for many years. A variety of research projects have indicated strong links between auditory factors and reading development.[7] The work of Peter Bryant and Lynette Bradley at Oxford in the 1980s drew attention to the phonological aspects of these links, related to the speech sounds (phonemes) of language and in particular to children's abilities to detect rhyme and alliteration at an early age. Usha Goswami discusses her subsequent research, first at Oxford and subsequently at Cambridge, in Chapter 4.

RHYME IN CHILDREN'S WRITING

The use of rhyme in children's writing raises other issues. Children's early reading can benefit from the phonological insights gained from experimenting in writing with word families.[8] But when writing fluency develops, many children – and adults – find that it is difficult to balance the theme of the writing with the formal patterns of written verse. Many may share Benedick's sentiments in Shakespeare's *Much Ado About Nothing;* '.. I cannot show it in rime; I have tried:.... no, I was not born under a riming planet'.[9] (This use of the word 'rime' differs from that of Usha Goswami in Chapter 4.) Sandy Brownjohn in Chapter 5 shows how good teaching can overcome such astrological defeatism, by coaching children in a number of subtle techniques and helping them to build up their linguistic skills and insights. She deals with other poetic forms, too, including alliteration. It is interesting to note that, before Chaucer's time, poets preferred this kind of 'head-rhyme' and that 'end-rhymes' only came into English poetry from the second half of the fourteenth century onwards.[10]

RHYMING VERSE FOR CHILDREN

There appears to be less contention about rhyming verse for children. Reading rhyme to children at home and school builds upon the early experiences which nursery rhymes have provided. Being read good rhyming verse brings satisfactions which reflect the very essence of poetry. As Ronald Tamplin points out, many poets are reassured by perceptible shape and structure, and rhyme is one of the strongest shape-giving devices.[11] The responsive young reader or listener is likely to gain similar satisfaction from rhyme's chiming recurrence. There are books which have been compiled to broaden children's experiences to other kinds of verse, such as Gerard Benson's *This Poem Doesn't Rhyme.*[12] This imaginative anthology ranges beyond rhyme to include alliteration, assonance, haiku, shape poems and riddles.

However, Brian Morse in Chapter 6 writes that rhyme has been widely used in verse which has been written for children and he provides a very wide-ranging review of its trends and features. The chapter needs to be set against the findings from the evaluation of the National Curriculum's implementation in 1991–3.[13] In a survey of 560 teachers of children in the 7–11 age-range, only one volume of poetry was mentioned by ten or more teachers as something which they made sure that their children read. The same volume was referred to by teachers of 7–8 year olds, 8–9 year olds and 9–10 year olds: Allan Ahlberg's *Please, Mrs Butler*[14] (no volume had ten or more mentions for 10–11 year olds). Brian Morse's chapter may help in promoting a use of poetry substantially beyond of Allan Ahlberg's humorous poetry on primary school life.

RIME STABILITY AND SPECIAL NEEDS

The rhyming features of English have also been recently exploited in provision for children with special educational needs. Frances James in Chapter 7 describes some pioneering work in one local education authority. Underpinning this work is the recognition that the notorious sound-letter relationships in written English are far more consistent in the letter strings which are found in '*rimes*', the rhyming parts of syllables. This 'rime stability' was noted by Marilyn Jager Adams in her major review of reading research, *Beginning to Read*, in 1990, which was commissioned by the USA Congress. She notes the finding that nearly 500 simple words can be derived from a set of only 37 rimes, for example: -ash, -est, -ick, -op and –ump.[15] By being helped to attend to rimes in this way, children may be helped to use analogies with known words to read relatively unfamiliar words. There are several other issues which need also to be borne in mind in helping to promote reading in this way. In order to use analogies productively, children may need first to have at least some decoding skills.[16] In addition, the quality of the text needs careful consideration. Many of the *Dr. Seuss* books[17] provide a promising combination of word play and zany entertainment in this context.

RHYMES AND CHANGING TIMES

Rhyme and other forms of word play have been part of our linguistic culture for centuries. Our most distinguished scholars in this area have been Peter and Iona Opie, who documented the variations and origins of over 1000 rhymes and jingles, some of which could be traced back over centuries.[18] *Rhyme, Reading and Writing* ends with a chapter on the Opies' work, written by Georgina Boyes, who has worked extensively with them. Among the questions which she addresses are how far our children live in a culture of rhyme and related word play: what distinguishes the lore and language of today's children?

MEMORABILITY AND MEANING

Word play in rhyme, as it does in rhythm, provides the enjoyment and satisfaction which come from other kinds of play; it can also help to make communication more memorable. We may recall snatches of word play which are linked to moments of insight and enduring pleasure. I remember, for instance, the delight when one of my primary school teachers illustrated the idea of alliteration by reciting the following doggerel:

> *Take two tremendous tigers,*
> *Tie tight their tails together,*
> *Tenderly tickle their toe-nails,*
> *'Til totally tire their temper.*

I recall the thrill of realisation at secondary school when a student teacher explained Wilfred Owen's use of consonance in the poem 'Strange Meeting', of which there is an extract in Tom McArthur's chapter. As a teacher myself, I remember marvelling at the poetic craft of Charles Causley and the way he uses rhyme in his ballads for children (further discussed by Brian Morse in Chapter 6). Such recollections are explained by what Tom McArthur indicates in the title to Chapter 2, that there is a kind of 'power' in patterned sound.

PERSPECTIVES ON RHYME, READING AND WRITING

Tom McArthur sets his discussion of 'Rhythm, rhyme and reason' in the context of the evolution of mammals and humans. He shows how anatomical and neural developments enabled humans to produce a greater range of sounds than is produced by other creatures. Before the use of written symbols, this repertoire of vowels, consonants, syllables and melodies was used to pass on knowledge by using various mnemonic and delivery techniques, including rhythm and rhyme.

Tom McArthur distinguishes between two senses of the term rhyme, what he calls 'rhyme-1' (sound play in general) and 'rhyme-2' (the everyday meaning in present-day English). He shows how this distinction helps to clarify historical overlaps in definition and goes on to show how alliteration has had a wider range of use, from verse to newspaper headlines. While rhyme may not have the same range, it is more complex. The chapter sets out the principal ways of achieving rhyme between words and phrases, illustrations of the main technical vocabulary which is associated with it and examples of some rhyme schemes.

The chapter ends with a note on the curious fact that, despite the vast amount of rhymed verse in English, the language is not rich in rhymable words, because it lacks the complex recurring inflections of languages like Italian and Spanish. It shows how English writers have coped with this and how rhyme can be combined within the repertoire of the sound play to which small children gleefully discover that they are heirs.

Marian Whitehead takes up the theme of gleeful discovery in her chapter on Nonsense, Rhyme and Word Play in Young Children. She combines extracts from children's word play and snippets of traditional rhymes with a wide-ranging discussion of research and publications in the field. She shows how investigations into young children's word play can provide insights into childhood, language and the workings of the human mind.

The chapter draws inspiration from Kornei Chukovsky's seminal work *From Two to Five*, which Marian Whitehead describes as 'crammed with stunning evidence of children's thinking and linguistic creativity'. She also notes that Chukovsky draws attention to the way in which children delight in overturning conventional ideas as they experiment with language in coming to terms with 'reality'. (This radical edge of word play is also taken up in Georgina Boyes' chapter and her review of the work of Peter and Iona Opie.) Marian Whitehead goes on to discuss various aspects of children's 'language play' and the part played by metaphors and role play in this process. She notes how selective and exaggerated such role play can be and how the use of props or 'pivots' can support it. The chapter continues by reminding us of the continuing importance of narrative in shaping and understanding new experience and re-affirms how children explore the meanings of words and language in playful ways. Children also enjoy subverting popular songs, poems and the like, an activity which is sometimes referred to as 'carnival', in the light of the parody, role-reversal and even sexual licence which can be included. Again, this subversion is reflected in some of the examples which appear in Georgina Boyes' chapter. Such subversion through language use can have a 'defusing', as well as an exploitive, aspect, a kind of 'deep play', which may be therapeutic in confronting 'worst-case scenarios'.

Like Tom McArthur in the previous chapter, Marian Whitehead shows how the raw material of poetry is present in children's earliest learning, as they repeat and re-order sounds and words, sometimes in an open-ended way and sometimes to capture the essential feeling of experience. All this suggests that nursery rhymes, poetry, nonsense verse, tongue-twisters, and other aspects of word play should be central features of an early years curriculum. The following chapter by Usha Goswami shows how this experience can be exploited in helping children to become aware of the phonological features of alliteration, onsets and rimes.

Usha Goswami sets her chapter in the context of children's traditional pleasure from hearing and sharing nursery rhymes and of their contemporary knowledge of advertising jingles and pop songs. Running through her chapter are certain distinctions between the different aspects of children's learning of the phonology of the language, its sound system. These distinctions include syllables and the units of syllables, the rhyming part (the 'rime') and, if there is one, the preceding consonant sound (the 'onset'). She confirms that there is a strong and specific connection between early rhyming and later reading development and summarises how children's spontaneous use of rhyme is reflected in their performance in experimental rhyme detection tasks. The chapter then goes on to summarise research findings on the degree of phonemic similarity between rhyming words and others, with a recommendation on how early years teachers might draw children's attention to which words in nursery rhymes do and do not rhyme. The chapter describes how predictive links and causal connections between rhyme awareness and learning to read have been found, in longitudinal studies and in studies of children whose reading development is delayed.

Usha Goswami cites evidence to show how the English spelling patterns are far more consistent in relation to its rimes than they are in relation to its phoneme-grapheme ('sound-letter') relationships. This 'rime stability' can help children in learning to read by enabling them to use analogies in reading words which share letter strings. In learning to read, children are able to use rime analogies before analogies based on other kinds of shared spelling units in words. Children's use of rime analogies is related to their rhyming skill. The research reviewed in the chapter enables a causal-developmental model of learning to read to be drawn up and this is set out in Figure 4.1. She notes that the research has not directly addressed the question of when teaching of individual letter-sound connections should occur, although she suggests that phonemic awareness appears to be a consequence of being taught to read. Awareness of syllables and of the within-syllable units of onsets and rimes, on the other hand, emerges prior to knowledge about phonemes. The influence of learning to read on phonemic awareness is demonstrated in research on adult illiterates.

Clearly this a complex area and it is not easy to disentangle the studies of phonological development *per se* and interest in how this research relates to the teaching of early reading. However, this chapter has clear practical implications for early childhood education: extensive informal experience of rhymes and singing games and, where appropriate, more directed attention to the recognition of rhyming words and alliteration. Usha Goswami also recommends that, in the teaching of early reading, emphasis can be given to the links between rhyming sounds and their spelling sequences and also between alliterative 'families' of words and the letters which they represent. These emphases may be less confusing for beginning readers than letter-by-letter decoding. She also recommends a substantial use of rhyming books with rhyming texts, with analogies being modelled for children by the use of resources such as plastic letters.

The focus of **Sandy Brownjohn's** chapter is on children writing poetry. She shows how children can be constrained in their writing because of preconceptions that poems always have to rhyme. This is understandable because of the 'lure' of memorable language features to which other chapters refer, but there is also a strong case for teaching the techniques which are central to the craft of poetic writing. The chapter outlines some ways of developing explicit knowledge of this

craft in teachers and children. It shows how forms of
repetition can be consciously used in combination with subtle
changes of words and meanings and it illustrates the way forms
first introduced in Tom McArthur's chapter appear in various
nursery rhymes. Sandy Brownjohn also shows how variations
from 'end-stop rhymes' can be used, internally within lines in
assonance, consonance and alliteration.

In going on to classroom practices, the chapter warns against
trying to do too much too soon, as the demand of balancing
rhythm, rhyme and meaning can prove too much for some
children. If rhyme is initially avoided in writing poetry, other
poetic forms can first be encouraged, for instance haiku, tanka
and cinquains, as these can help children to be confident and
adventurous. Verbal dexterity in using full rhyme can come
from oral and written games, some of which draw upon the
onsets and rimes discussed by Usha Goswami in the previous
chapter. Examples of assonance and consonance may occur
naturally but unconsciously in children's writing and insightful
teachers can point these out. The chapter ends with some
intriguing examples of children consciously using different
rhyming forms. Sandy Brownjohn argues that such proficiency
can allow more technical rhyming forms to be tackled, thus
helping children to experience the sense of power and
confidence from being able to use the 'best words in the best
order'.

Brian Morse provides a richly informative survey of adult
writers who have successfully put the best words in the best
order for children to read. He suggests that poetry written for
children has consistently used rhyme and that the
'modernising' trends of the late 1970s have generally not been
maintained. The chapter draws attention to the special nature
of poetry and to the kind of reading which it involves. There
are important implications for how children can be
encouraged to tackle the distinctive nature of such textual
experiences, which can vary so much from poem to poem and
page to page. Children will appreciate a poem better by
learning a little about the history and culture of the times
when it was written. They will become more aware of the
interplay of rhythm, rhyme and meaning by being helped to
do full justice to these aspects when reading out loud.

The chapter goes on to review the trends in provision of poetry in primary schools, from the once ubiquitous *Child's Garden of Verses* to the currently ubiquitous *Please, Mrs Butler*. He draws attention to some less well-known poets from the Victorian period and comments on some of the poetic achievements in writing for the early years, 8–12-year-olds and for older children. He uses 1970 as a watershed, in recognition of the significance of Charles Causley's *Figgie Hobbin* and of the special qualities which this volume represents. Brian Morse makes a wealth of references to poets, poems and the themes which are written about, helpfully adding his own views to promote discussion and debate. The chapter gives a clear indication of the legacy which can be exploited in bringing children and rhyme together.

Frances James reports on how children and rhyme have been brought together in helping to meet children's special needs in reading and spelling in the Suffolk local education authority. She relates her work to the model of the four psychological 'processors' which are integrally involved in reading, according to Marilyn Jager Adams, those involving meaning and context, together with visual and phonological processors. The chapter is particularly concerned with the latter, but it stresses that the teaching of reading should reflect the use of all four.

Like Usha Goswami's chapter, that by Frances James is influenced by the work at Oxford University in the 1980s which confirmed the link between children's recognition of rhyme and alliteration and their reading attainment. The work promoted new teaching techniques in Suffolk which are reported in detail in the chapter. Two nursery schools specifically promoted general language skills and two specifically promoted appreciation of rhyme, with the children being assessed beforehand and subsequently. The assessment procedures included standardised and specially developed criterion-referenced assessments of children's knowledge of nursery rhymes. Some intended assessments were found not to be satisfactory because of limits in children's short-term memory and in their understanding of the term 'odd one out'. Instead, a picture task was used.

The chapter also refers to links between the Suffolk project and work elsewhere. The curriculum activities which have been developed in the project are described in detail: general auditory awareness; recognition of oral rhyme; recognition of rhyming words which share the same spelling pattern; developing analogies by using plastic letters. Frances James summarises the progress of the project and where it might now lead. Her chapter indicates how an awareness of the significance of rhyme and alliteration can be of considerable help when providing for children with special needs.

The final chapter by **Georgina Boyes** explores the legacy of the work of Iona and Peter Opie, whose survey of the rhymes and word play of 5000 children resulted in the seminal *Lore and Language of Schoolchildren* in 1959. The chapter begins with a reminder of the Opies' achievement in showing how children's rhymes were part of a dynamic oral heritage, in which history and modernity existed side by side. At the same time, the scale of the Opies' achievement has to be set against the limitations of their methodology, particularly the gatekeeper role of teachers and publishers in relation to 'dubious' material. The use of the word 'knickers' apparently demarcated the boundary of acceptability. Paradoxically, the content of some enduring rhymes is now more likely to be challenged on grounds of 'political correctness' or because of the way they apparently condone violence and impropriety. Georgina Boyes reminds us that any analysis of 'acceptability' has to be placed in the context of children's culture, being an expression of their own beliefs, values and enjoyment. The remainder of the chapter explores the 'lore and language' of today's children in the context of their own unselfconscious culture.

Despite the pessimism of commentators, the chapter provides convincing evidence of children's continuing ability to create new rhymes and to adapt old ones. It suggests that the persistence of game rhymes reflects developmental and cultural influences, as well as a widely shared delight in language, rhythm and rhyme. Several examples are given of how game rhymes have been reworked to include new fads and fashions, although it remains a mystery why some snatches and jingles enter and survive in the lore of the playground. But, whatever explanations are put forward, the cultural processes identified by the Opies in the way children create and communicate rhymes seem to be operating as securely today as in the past.

A WIDER SIGNIFICANCE

Summarising the contents of *Rhyme, Reading and Writing* in this way provides a clear indication of how its contributors have shed light on some of the issues which were mentioned earlier. The book also has a wider significance. It indicates what can be achieved in a synthesis of insights from the different disciplines of linguistics, psychology and literature. This synthesis can help to compensate for the inevitably sketchy references to rhyme in documents like the National Curriculum for English.

The specific focus on rhyme also serves an additional function. Recent years have seen a great deal of attention being given to narrative prose and the support which this can give young readers and writers. But the emphasis has tended to be on the semantic and syntactic aspects of language. Attention to rhyme ensures that there is emphasis on the phonological aspects, too. In the words of Linda Hall, author of one of the most positive and wide-ranging books on poetry teaching, attention to rhyme can explore how 'sound, sense, rhyme, and images all work together in a unity to appeal to our understanding through our senses as well as our intellect'.[19] A growing appreciation of rhyme and word play can take us into the child's world of linguistic experimentation and into the realms of the distilled literature of our culture. This appreciation can lead to an awareness of the phonemic structure of language and of the ways children can learn to use it in reading and spelling. Parents, teachers and all who care for young children can be helped to exploit the repetitions and resonance in the sounds which make up the repertoire of human language.

ACKNOWLEDGEMENTS

I am very grateful to Nicholas Bielby, Jane Oakhill and my wife, Jenny, for reading and commenting upon a draft of this chapter. I do, of course, take full responsibility for the final version.

$\mathscr{R}$EFERENCES

1. From Chukovsky, K. (1968) *From Two To Five*, revised edition, translated by Miriam Morton. Berkeley and Los Angeles: University of California Press, p.99

2. Halliwell, J.O. (1853) *The Nursery Rhymes of England.* London: The Bodley Head

3. Department of Education and Science (1975) *A Language for Life (The Bullock Report)*. London: Her Majesty's Stationery Office, p.85

4. See, for example, Bryant, P. and Bradley, L. (1985) *Children's Reading Problems.* Oxford: Basil Blackwell; and Goswami, U. and Bradley, P. (1990) *Phonological Skills and Learning to Read.* Hove: Lawrence Erlbaum Associates

5. See Note 1.

6. Chukovsky, K. (1968) *From Two To Five*, revised edition, translated by Miriam Morton. Berkeley and Los Angeles: University of California Press, pp.89–90

7. See, for example, Department of Education and Science (1975) *A Language for Life (The Bullock Report)*. London: Her Majesty's Stationery Office, Chapter 18

8. See, for example, Adams, M.J. (1990) *Beginning to Read.* Cambridge, Mass.: MIT Press, esp. Chapter 15; and Clay, M.M. (1991) *Becoming Literate.* Auckland, NZ: Heinemann Education, esp. Chapter 5

9. William Shakespeare, *Much Ado About Nothing*, Act V, Scene ii

10. Reeves, J. (1965) *Understanding Poetry.* London: Heinemann, p.150

11. Tamplin, R. (1993) *Rhythm and Rhyme.* Buckingham: Open University Press, p.13

12. Benson, G. (Ed.) (1992) *This Poem Doesn't Rhyme.* London: Puffin/Penguin Books

13. Raban, B., Clark, U. and McIntyre, J. (1994) *Evaluation of the Implementation of English in the National Curriculum at Key Stages 1, 2 and 3 (1991–1993)*. London: School Curriculum and Assessment Authority

14. Ahlberg, A. (1984) *Please Mrs Butler.* Harmondsworth: Puffin/Penguin Books

15. Adams, M.J. (1990) *Beginning to Read.* Cambridge, Mass.: MIT Press, Chapter 12

16. See, for instance, Ehri, L.C. and Robbins, C. (1992) 'Beginners need some decoding skill to read words by analogy', in *Reading Research Quarterly*, 27, 1, 13–26
17. The *Dr. Seuss* books are published in the United Kingdom by Collins Educational
18. Opie, I. and Opie, P. (1951) *The Oxford Dictionary of Nursery Rhymes*. Oxford: Oxford University Press; and Opie, I. and Opie, P. (1963) *The Puffin Book of Nursery Rhymes*. Harmondsworth: Puffin/Penguin Books
19. Hall, L. (1989) *Poetry for Life*. London: Cassell, p.14

2

※※※※※※※※※※※※※※※※※※※※※※※※※※※※※※※※※※※※※

RHYTHM, RHYME AND REASON: THE POWER OF PATTERNED SOUND

Tom McArthur

> *Mr. Fox!*
> *I hate this game, Sir.*
> *This game makes*
> *my tongue quite lame, sir.*
> *Mr. Knox, sir,*
> *That's a shame, sir.*
> *We'll find something*
> *new to do now.*
> *Here is lots of*
> *new blue goo now.*
> *New goo. Blue goo.*
> *Gooey. Gooey.*
> *Blue goo. New goo.*
> *Gluey. Gluey.*[1]

All language began as sound. Nowadays, although we can read, write, print, type and word-process, language is still primarily vocal and auditory: anything dumbly visual can be turned 'back' into vocal sound by anyone at any time, either out loud or in the mind. In addition, 'fossilised' patterns of talk, recitation, chanting and song survive in all written languages from the now silent ages before script was known. These patterns infect every text ever composed or likely to be composed and the infection takes many forms, not least of which are rhythm and rhyme.

THE BEGINNINGS OF SPEECH

Vocal sound appears to have originated in the service of the very young some 250 million years ago, when the first mammals evolved. At least four attributes mark off the mammalia from all earlier life forms, two of them directly relating to communication:

- Their females feed their young from glands that produce milk.
- Their young can all instinctively produce the 'mammalian isolation cry'.
- Their young take a long time to mature.
- They all have a 'middle ear', a facility that enables them to hear such plaintive sounds as the mammalian isolation cry.

Because of the way they are fed, recently born mammals need to stay close to their mother. To help them do this they produce, whether they are mice, bats, bears, humans, or anything else, specific small plaintive sounds. They can make these sounds because they have a larynx, an organ in the throat that first evolved in reptiles, not for the sake of sound at all but as a valve to close and protect the lungs from foreign matter. Mammals, however, can also use the larynx to cough and make communicative sounds.

Apes, which evolved some 70 million years ago, make a wide range of sounds compared with most earlier mammals. As in those earlier mammals, the ape's larynx is at the back of the mouth, a location that allows for swallowing and breathing at the same time. In addition, an ape's tongue is rooted in the mouth. These features also appear to have been true of Australopithecus, a genus with both ape-like and proto-human attributes that lived in Africa some four million years ago, but not true of the first members of the genus *Homo*, or any later humans. In addition to having larger brains than apes and australopithecines, humans have larynxes that are located behind the mouth during the childhood years, as with other mammals, but move downwards as the years pass to an adult position in mid-throat. In addition, human babies have the tongue rooted in the mouth, like apes, but in older children and adults it is rooted in the pharynx, the cavity behind the mouth. Both developments allow a much greater vocal freedom than in any earlier mammal.[2]

These anatomical adaptations occurred in lockstep, as it were, with the neural developments (especially the left hemisphere of the brain) that make possible complex muscular movements in the mouth and throat and also in the dominant hand (usually the right). Such changes have not only made complex speech possible, but have also laid the foundation for the intricacies of writing; an expression of manual dexterity. It is an intriguing feature of evolution that there were physiological links between brain, mouth and hand long before language became a dual tool, with speech and writing: indeed, before it became a triple tool, with speech, writing and gestural signing for the deaf.

However, the various adaptations in larynx and tongue have not been entirely beneficial. Because of the altered position of the larynx, adult humans cannot swallow and breathe at the same time: they choke if they try. Because of adaptations to mouth and jaw, chewing is harder for humans than for apes, and the impacted wisdom teeth to which humans are prone can often have serious consequences. Nevertheless, the anatomy and physiology of our heads and necks, our lowered larynx, and a tongue rooted in the pharynx together make possible a range of sound beyond the ability of any other living creature. This range includes the production of:

- syllables: short composite sounds whose flow is generated by air pulses from the lung;
- vowels and consonants: contrastive 'atoms' of sound produced in the mouth and pharynx that make up the phonetic content of syllables (singly or in groups);
- patterns of rhythm and modulation;
- a continuum of melody with, for most cultures, talk at one end and song at the other.

These, one can say, constitute the evolutionary building blocks from which the physical structures of language (spoken, chanted and sung) have emerged. The sensory, analytical and directive apparatus of the brain provide the syntactic and semantic complex with which such physical structures mesh smoothly. The first and still primary outcome of this development has been a vast and intricate range of oral performance. Long before the means were available to store information beyond the brain (on wood, stone, clay tablets, papyrus sheets and other surfaces) the first singers, chanters, reciters and orators developed mnemonic and delivery techniques to help them remember and pass on their knowledge and make it as easy as possible for their listeners to understand and remember what was heard. With the exception of ancillary facial expressions and manual gestures, everything was oral and aural: the need was to find ways of achieving something as permanent as possible by means of an entirely transient medium.

The resulting 'storage speech', which survives in full only in non-literate societies, is ancestral to many devices used in theatres and schools, such as verse patterns, stock formulas, aids to rote learning and rhetorical tropes (such as playing with sounds and using figures of speech). Ancient singers, chanters and reciters formalised the patterns of sound and meaning already present in ordinary language so as to develop techniques for remembering and reciting their community records, for performing social rituals (individual and choral), for narrating stories and for singing work songs. Prominent among the tricks of this ancient oral trade were devices associated with the way in which vocal sound 'flows'.[3]

RHYTHM

The English word *rhythm* derives through Latin *rhythmus* from Greek *rhuthmós*, which means 'flow', and especially 'measured flow'. The basic concept, image or metaphor/simile of sounds that flow as if they were water is very old, and has been used and understood in slightly different ways in such fields as acoustics, music, poetics and phonetics, bringing in such further images and models as 'sound is like a wave', 'sound has a beat', 'sounds are long or short' and 'voices move'.

- **In acoustics** Rhythm is wave-like, with a steady beat and elements of longer and shorter duration.
- **In music** Rhythm consists of beats and lengths of notes shown as bars (groups of beats), the first beat of each bar being stressed.
- **In poetics** Rhythm is the arrangement of syllables in more or less regular sequences of two types of verse: in languages like Latin, these are usually sequences of syllables that contain longer or shorter vowels (*quantitative metre*); in

languages like English, they are usually sequences of stressed and unstressed syllables (*accentual metre*).
* **In phonetics** Rhythm is vocal movement created by the stress, quantity, and timing of syllables.

There is nothing more fundamental to a language than its rhythm: it is one of the first features to be acquired by children and one of the most difficult for adults to change, or to adopt convincingly in another language. The rhythm of language begins in the lungs, in pulses of air produced by the movement of the intercostal respiratory muscles. Phoneticians have three terms for such pulses: *chest pulses, breath pulses* and *syllable pulses.* A flow of such pulses (the foundation for syllables) produces the beat heard in all normal speech. The rest of a syllable (the phonetic qualities that distinguish, say, *hi* from *ho, ba* from *ka*) is as it were added in the mouth, in association with pharynx and nose. However, sometimes a pulse can occur without producing any sound at all, as for example when one says '*kyou* instead of *thank you,* a condition known as *silent stress,* in which there is still a beat even though the syllable, in this case *than,* is not pronounced. A chest pulse with greater force than usual is called a *stress pulse,* which is realised in speech as a stressed syllable. Ordinary chest pulses occur at about five per second, stress pulses less frequently.

The two kinds of pulse work differently together in different languages, producing distinctive rhythms. Phoneticians, seeking to account for differences in the timing of elements in different languages, distinguish two types: *syllable-timed* and *stress-timed* languages, depending on whether the unit of time is the syllable or the foot. Some languages fit well into these categories; others do not. Syllable-timed languages, which include French and Japanese, have a characteristic *rat-a-tat* beat, each syllable equal; stress-timed languages, which include English and Russian, have a characteristic *TUMpty-TUMpty-TUM* beat, some elements more prominent than others. Among the languages that do not fit neatly are Arabic and Hindi, and timing is in any case not uniform throughout speech in any language, for many reasons, including simply the wish on certain occasions to do things differently.

The two categories are therefore useful fictions rather than absolute facts, but the distinction has sound pedagogical value when, for example, speakers of English aim for syllable-timing in their French and speakers of French aim for stress-timing in their English. Importantly, whatever kind of rhythm a language has, it will generally be more marked in recitation, chanting and song, as part of that language's tradition of storage speech, and this is true for everything from epic recitals to nursery rhymes. And the ancient implications of storage speech will carry over into the reading of texts.

A noteworthy feature of rhythm in English is the reduction of the vowels in unstressed (weak) syllables towards a centralising vowel, known as *schwa* and represented in phonetic script by the symbol [ə]. A gentle cough-like sound, as in the first syllable of *above* and the second syllable of *organise,* schwa is the commonest vowel sound in the language. Often the reduction of the substance in an unstressed syllable is so great that there is no vowel at all. Instead, there is a *syllabic consonant,* such as a syllabic [n] in the second spoken syllable of *happen* and a syllabic [l] in the second spoken syllable of *little.*

The standard orthography of English provides no clues about the rhythm of speech, especially rapid speech. There are no graphic devices for displaying inequality among spoken syllables, with the exception of certain conventions of colloquiality and verse: for example, when an apostrophe marks the loss of a sound, as in *don't* for *do not* and *cap'n* for *captain.* It is therefore important for both children and adults learning to read English to know about rhythms that are not reflected in print, and to come to terms with them, usually by oral practice and a comparison of text and sound (for example, while listening to living exemplars and/or to recordings). Native-speaking children of course have a great advantage over non-native-speaking children and adult learners, because they have learned the rhythms long before going to school. But they too need help with relating what they know, and can do 'naturally', to what they find on a printed page or screen. In a serious sense, when they learn to read they have to learn to supply the rhythm that is there but cannot be seen.[4]

RHYTHM AND RHYME

The resemblance between the words *rhythm* and *rhyme* is not accidental. They come from the same etymological stable as do *frail* and *fragile*, *royal* and *regal*, and other such doublets: paired words with similar histories, forms and meanings. English is particularly rich in doublets because Latin words have often come into the language along two routes:

- indirectly through French (usually at an earlier time);
- directly from Latin (usually at a later time).

For example, while *frail* came from French, considerably adapting the Latin original *fragilis* (meaning 'breakable'), *fragile* came directly from the Latin and so resembles it much more closely; similarly, *royal* came through French, but *regal* came directly from *regalis* ('kingly'). Comparably, *rhyme* came through French, earlier, and *rhythm* came directly from Latin, much later. Both are from *rhythmus*, which, as noted above, had already been taken into Latin from Greek. That is a complex enough state of affairs, but the story has been further complicated by the vagaries of medieval orthography and collisions and separations of meaning.

In medieval Latin, the term *rhythmus* (usually spelled *rythmus* or *rithmus*) was not generally used in the classical sense of 'a measured flow of sound' but in three senses relating to *consonance*, as (1) the harmony or correspondence of sounds of any kind (as opposed to *dissonance*, disharmony), and (2) especially the harmony of consonants (as opposed to *assonance*, the harmony of vowels), and (3) especially the harmony of consonants at the ends of words, as in the Latin phrases:

- *beati pacifici* ('blessed [are] the peace-makers'), where the same plural ending *-i* occurs twice;
- *verbatim et litteratim* ('word for word and letter for letter': that is, accurately rendered), where the same adverbial ending *-atim* occurs twice;
- *dabit qui dedit* ('he will give [again] who has [already] given), where the same third-person ending *-it* occurs twice, and there is also alliteration with *d*.

Patterns of this kind, also referred to in the classical tradition as *homeoteleuton* (Greek: '[something with] the same ending [as something else]'), were common in Latin because of its wide range of inflectional word endings. Such patterns are closely comparable to what people recognise as *rhyme* in present-day English, but are not the same, because rhyme in English depends on syllables and parts of syllables without reference to function or meaning, *not* on elements in words that are the same because they have the same function or the same meaning. In the Middle Ages, therefore, Latin *rhythmus*, although directly ancestral to English *rhythm*, did not have its present-day meaning, but meant something closer to present-day *rhyme*, of which it was the indirect ancestor.

The medieval Latin forms *rythmus* and *rithmus* were the source of the Old French noun *rime*, first used in the twelfth century. The meaning of *rime* was the same as Latin *rythmus/rithmus*, 'consonance, particularly in the endings of two or more words', but this was extended by the thirteenth century to include verse that contains such consonance of endings – and the type of verse that was particularly noted for 'rime' had accentual rather than quantitative metre: something far commoner in English than in Latin. In this we have the beginning of the recognition of our *rhyme* and perhaps also a greater use of techniques that we can recognise as rhyme.

In the sixteenth century, Latin *rhythmus* was adapted into French as *rhythme* and came either directly or through French into English, with a very wide range of spelling, including at least *rithme, rhithme, rythme, rhythme, rithm, rhithm, rythm, rhythm* (all generally pronounced 'rime'). The term had at that time two meanings:

- all the senses of medieval *rithmus* and *rime*, relating to consonance, especially of endings; in other words, it subsumed the meanings of *rime*;
- the classical, and present-day, sense of 'measured flow'.

The old spelling *rime* had continued unchallenged until this time when, in addition to a flood of new words from Latin and Greek, there was a massive re-Latinisation of words borrowed from Latin in earlier times. Because they had mainly been borrowed through French they had a distinctly un-Latin look and sound, which the Latinisers felt ought to be rectified. In French, *rime* has kept its ancient indigenous spelling and pronunciation, but in English there was pressure to conform to a classical norm on the printed page whether or not people kept the old pronunciation. After 1600, however, two compromise spellings emerged, each adding an *h* to *rime* but not a *t* or a *th*. These were *rhime* and *rhyme*. The second prevailed because of the strong Greek associations of the *y*: compare *hypnosis, psychic, syzygy*. The older form *rime* has, however, continued as a minority practice, favoured by some because it is the older form or is easier to spell, or both. It is also universally accepted in certain contexts, such as the full title of Samuel Taylor Coleridge's poem *The Rime of the Ancient Mariner*. (In Chapter 4, Usha Goswami uses the term 'rime' to refer to the unit that reflects the rhyming sound in two words.)

The words *rhyme* and *rhythm*, then, collided in the sixteenth century, an age of great oral and orthographic flux, and for a time the written form *rhythm* had the fundamental meaning of both words as used today. By the seventeenth century, however, *rhythm* was restricted to the flow of poetry, by the nineteenth its range expanded to include the flow of prose, and by the twentieth it covered all the measured flow detectable in the universe, from language and music to wholesale physical and social movement and change. And, most importantly for our purposes, by the seventeenth century the pair *rhythm* and *rhyme* had been established, with separate spelling, pronunciations and areas of meaning.[5]

RHYME-1 AND RHYME-2

Rhythm is clearly a universal of language, but the status of rhyme is not so clear: or at least not of *rhyme* as the term is generally understood at the present time in English. It may, however, be possible to borrow from and in effect formalise the medieval sense of *rime*, proposing as a result two senses of *rhyme* that we can bear in mind today, the first containing the second, as follows:

• **Rhyme-1** a broader sense that can also be called *sound play*, covering all the echoes, chimes and resonances of language. Rhyme-1 includes such phenomena as alliteration, consonance, assonance and homeoteleuton (words having the same endings), as well as all the other aesthetic, euphoric, stylistic and rhetorical devices that, as it were, sit 'on top of' rhythm, giving it added value. In this containing sense, rhyme *is* a universal of language, expressed differently in different languages. Whereas rhythm starts in the lungs, rhyme-1 belongs in the vocal apparatus of mouth, pharynx and nose. In its echoic, chiming, mnemonic way it is as fundamental as rhythm or syntax or any other aspect of speech.

- **Rhyme-2** a narrower sense, covering only one realisation of rhyme-1, and therefore on a par with alliteration, assonance and the other subtypes just listed. Rhyme-2 has the everyday meaning of rhyme in present-day English: 'identity in sound of some part, esp[ecially] the end, of words or lines of verse' (the first sense of the entry *rhyme* in *The Random House Dictionary of the English Language,* second edition, unabridged, 1987). Rhyme-2 is only one of many ways in which the language-universal rhyme-1 is realised in a particular language or cultural tradition at any time.

This division, and its close association with rhythm, helps resolve various problematical aspects of the term *rhyme.* For example, Clark and Whitehall (1974)[6] have commented as follows on both the medieval coverage of *rhyme* and the lack of universality in what it primarily refers to today:

> To trace the history of r[hyme] in Western Atlantic literatures is a discursion into the unknown, particularly since early writers integrate it with assonance, consonance, alliteration and the like under one head. In native North America, it occurs only in one Indian language, where it is probably borrowed from Eng[lish]. Most cultures' verse lacks r[hyme] either as an organisational device or as ornament. (p.708)

> Systematic rhyming ... has appeared in such widely separated languages (e.g. Chinese, Sanskrit, Arabic, Norse, Prov[encal], Celtic) that its spontaneous development in more than one of them can be reasonably assumed. In the rest it may have been introduced like any other device from the outside, and any language that had already acquired r[hyme], no matter how, may have learned new applications of it from its neighbors. (p.706)

Use of the terms rhyme-1 and rhyme-2 helps clarify the difficulties to which Clark and Whitehall point. In the first quoted paragraph, the first sentence refers to rhyme-1, the second to rhyme-2, and we are free to suppose that other Native American languages have had other ways of embodying rhyme-1 (sound play, echoes, chimes) into their speech. The third sentence continues to discuss rhyme-2, indicating that it is not a universal feature of language. In the second paragraph, the first sentence also deals with limitations on rhyme-2: only some languages, exemplified by those listed, have rhyming verse comparable to that in English. The second sentence notes that such verse can spread from language to language through culture diffusion, and leaves undiscussed the question of what kinds of rhyme-1 (alliteration, etc.) already occur in languages that do not (yet) have rhyme-2.

Alliteration in english

Two aspects of rhyme-1 are particularly important in English, because of their high frequency of occurrence and their antithetical relationship: *alliteration*, which deals with similarity at the beginnings of words, such as the *b*s in *bread and butter* (and has for this reason sometimes been called *initial rhyme*) and *rhyme-2*, which concerns similarity at the ends of words, as with the *ings* in *ting-a-ling*. The two occur both independently of one another and in association, and each has dominated English verse at different times: alliteration in the Old English period (with a brief renaissance in Middle English), and rhyme-2 from the seventeenth to the earlier twentieth centuries. Alliteration has had a wider range of use than rhyme-2; the following list, adapted from the entry '*alliteration*' in *The Oxford Companion to the English Language* (1992)[7], identifies eleven areas in which it freely occurs:

- **Verse** 'O Wild West Wind, thou breath of autumn's being' (Shelley).
- **Story-telling prose** 'The great grey-green, greasy Limpopo River' (Kipling); 'Tune the pipes to the tragedy of tallow, the bane of bulk, the calamity of corpulence' (O. Henry).
- **Speech-making** 'Do not let us speak of darker days; let us rather speak of sterner days' (Churchill).
- **Advertising** 'Guinness is good for you'; 'You can be sure of Shell'.

- **Tongue-twisters** 'Peter Piper picked a peck of pickled peppers'; 'She sells sea-shells on the sea shore'.
- **Similes (often clichéd)** 'As cool as a cucumber'; 'as dead as a doornail'.
- **Reduplicated words** 'Flimflam'; 'Tittle-tattle'.
- **Collocations, idiomatic phrases and proverbs** 'Bed and breakfast'; 'Footloose and fancy-free'; 'Look before you leap'.
- **Nicknames and epithets** 'Battling Bill'; 'Tiny Tim'; 'The Broadway Butcher'.
- **Newspaper headlines (especially tabloid)** 'Saucy Sue brings home the bacon'.

The Companion also notes that alliteration is often for emphasis, to help drive a point home in a colourful and therefore memorable way, as in 'But Pooh is loved in Consett and Calgary, in Kalamazoo and Kalgoorlie, as tenderly as in Camberley and Carshalton' (Godfrey Hodgson, *The Independent*, 2 June 1990).

RHYME IN ENGLISH

Although it does not have the range of alliteration, rhyme-2 is more complex and has been thoroughly institutionalised. Like alliteration, one needs two or more words or phrases to achieve the desired effect, and a traditional term for these words and phrases is *rhyme fellows*. They are generally organised as follows:

- **monosyllabically** as in bold/gold;
- **disyllabically** (1) with stress on the second syllable, as in *amass/surpass*, and (2) with stress on the first syllable, as in *banter/canter*
- **trisyllabically** with initial stress, as in *battery/flattery*
- **phrasally** (1) with stress on the first words, as in *stayed with us/played with us* (2) with stress on the middle word, as in *you believe me/you deceive me*

Note Rhyme fellows of one sort may rhyme with those of another sort, as in *I'm a poet and I don't know it.*

Since the sixteenth century at least an extensive technical vocabulary has developed for discussing the mechanics of verse rhyming in English. The major terms in this vocabulary, with specimens, are:

- **End rhyme** (the commonest form) The occurrence of rhyming words at the end of lines of verse, as in the second and fourth lines of the following stanza, but not the first and third:

  > *'Is there anybody there?' said the Traveller,*
  > *Knocking on the moonlit* door,
  > *And his horse in the silence champ'd the grasses*
  > *Of the forest's ferny f*loor.
  > Walter de la Mare, The Listeners

Note The alliteration in *f* in the fourth line blends into the rhyme.

- **Internal/interior rhyme** The occurrence of rhyming words within a line of verse, either in their own right (first example) or with an internal word that rhymes with a terminal word (second example, in which the effect is of two short lines written as one):

  > *Sister, my sister, O* fleet sweet *swallow,*
  > *Thy way is long to the sun and south.*
  > Algernon Swinburne, Itylus

  > *Then a sentimental* passion *of a vegetable* fashion.
  > W.S. Gilbert, Patience

- **Masculine/single/strong rhyme** The occurrence of rhymed stressed syllables (often monosyllables and usually forming a noun, verb or adjective) at the ends of lines:

  > *Stands the Church clock at ten to* three?
  > *And is there honey still for* tea?
  > Rupert Brooke, The Old Vicarage, Grantchester

- **Feminine/double/weak rhyme** The occurrence of rhymes that include unstressed syllables following immediately after stressed syllables:

  > *Love is enough: though the World be a-wan*ing,
  > *And the woods have no voice but the voice of complain*ing.
  > William Morris, Love is enough

- **Triple rhyme** The (rare) occurrence in verse of rhymes that include two unstressed syllables coming immediately after stressed syllables:

  > *I'd rather have a* tricycle
  > *Than I would have a* bicycle,
  > *For skidding on an* icicle
  > *Is safer on a* tricycle.

  Anon

- **Eye/vision rhyme** The occurrence of what appears to be rhyme but is an illusion created by a resemblance in spelling or by a desire to force a rhyme because of such a resemblance:

  > *A creature might forget to weep who bore*
  > *Thy comfort long, and lose thy love* thereby!
  > *But love me for love's sake, that evermore*
  > *Thou mayst love on, through love's* eternity.

  Elizabeth Barrett Browning, *Sonnets from the Portuguese*

  > *A certified poet from* Slough,
  > *Whose methods of rhyming were* rough,.
  > *Retorted, 'I see*
  > *That the letters agree*
  > *And if that's not sufficient I'm* through'

  Limerick, Clifford Witting

- **Imperfect/near/half/oblique rhyme, pararhyme, off rhyme, slant rhyme** Terms, often with different meanings, for echoes at the ends of lines that do not fit the usual rhyme-2 patterns but belong nonetheless within the circle of rhyme-1, because they are kinds of assonance, consonance and the like. Three examples are provided without further analysis:

  > *It seemed that out of battle I* escaped
  > *Down some profound long tunnel, long since* scooped
  > *Through granites which titanic wars had* groined.
  > *Yet also there encumbered sleepers* groaned,
  > *Too fast in thought or death to be bestirred.*

  Wilfred Owen, *Strange Meeting*

> And when to the chase his court would crowd,
> The poor flung ploughshares on his road,
> And shrieked, 'Our cry is from King to God!'
>> Dante Gabriel Rossetti, *The White Ship*

>> One dignity delays for all
>> One mited Afternoon
>> None can avoid this purple
>> None evade this Crown!
>>> Emily Dickinson, 98

RHYME SCHEMES AND RHETORICAL DEVICES

The above description of rhyme fellows and kinds of rhyme demonstrates a high level of organisation and variation. There is, however, a higher level still, in which rhymes take on complex but stable patterns known as *rhyme schemes*. Such schemes have at least two functions: to provide the poet with a framework within which to work and to encourage in the reader or listener a degree of anticipation and even at times of prediction. The following three specimens are representative but by no means exhaustive, and their rhyme schemes are identified in the traditional way by means of letter formulas:

aabb

I will make you brooches and toys for your delight	a
Of bird-song at morning and star-shine at night.	a
I will make a palace fit for you and me,	b
Of green days in forests and blue days at sea.	b
I will make my kitchen, and you shall keep your room,	
Where white flows the river and bright blows the broom,	
And you shall wash your linen and keep your body white	
In rainful at morning and dewfall at night.	

> Robert Louis Stevenson, *Romance*

ababb

Helen, thy beauty is to me	a
Like those Nicean bards of yore	b
That gently, o'er the perfumed sea,	a

> The weary way-worn wanderer bore   b
> To his native shore.   b
>
> On desperate seas long wont to roam,
> Thy hyacinth hair, thy classic face,
> Thy Naiad airs have brought me home
> To the glory that was Greece,
> And the grandeur that was Rome.
>   Edgar Allen Poe, *To Helen*

abcb

> It is ancient Mariner,   a
> And he stoppeth one of three   b
> 'By thy long grey beard and glittering eye,   c
> Now wherefore stopp'st thou me?   b
>
> The Bridegroom's doors are open'd wide,
> And I am next of kin;
> The guests are met, the feast is set:
> May'st hear the merry din.'
>   Samuel Taylor Coleridge, *The Rime of the Ancient Mariner*

Together with specific metrical patterns, such as iambic pentameter (which I will not discuss here), such rhyme schemes often serve to identify kinds of *stanzas* (groups of lines of verse), as for example a four-line stanza rhyming *aabb*. Some stanza-identifying schemes are highly complex and varied, as for example the patterns of the sonnet, a genre that consists of only one stanza of 14 lines. One such rhyme scheme, used in Shakespeare's sonnet beginning 'Shall I compare thee to a summer's day', is *abab/cdcd/efef/gg*, embodied in the words:

> day, temperate, May, date   abab
> shines, dimmed, declines, untrimmed   cdcd
> fade, ow'st, shade, grow'st   efef
> see, thee   gg

In addition to its organisational role, rhyme-2 has a rhetorical role. For example in Shakespeare's plays, which are written almost entirely in blank (unrhymed) verse, a rhyming couplet is often, but not always, used to signal the end of a speech or a scene. Compare for example the last two lines of blank verse and then the closing couplet in the following, at the end of

Act 5, Scene 1 of *Romeo and Juliet.* Here a grief-stricken Romeo tells the apothecary to go, saying:

> *I sell thee poison; thou hast sold me none.*
> *Farewell, buy food, and get thyself in flesh.*
> *Come, cordial and not poison, go with me*
> *To Juliet's grave, for there must I use thee.*

It is curious that, despite the vast amount of rhymed verse in English (whether literary in the case of sonnets or general and popular in the case of nursery rhymes and pop songs), the language is not rich in rhymable words. English words are very different from those of more inflected languages like Italian and Spanish. Because they lack complex, recurring inflections, English words have a very wide range of endings, so that some rhyme fellows, like *mountain/fountain,* rhyme with no other words at all, short of nonsense words such as *plountain,* created in the spirit of Lewis Carroll and Dr Seuss simply so as produce a rhyme. Many words such as *breadth, circle* and *month,* have no rhyme fellows at all. Because of this, poets writing in English have freely made use of 'near rhymes' (known as *rhyming licences*) that involve assonance and other distant chimes, as in the above examples from the work of Owen, Rossetti, and Dickinson (under *imperfect rhyme*). Such ploys are acceptable (though only just) because there is simply so little to choose from. And for the same reason certain kinds of romantic and popular verse lean heavily on such clichéd rhyme fellows as *moon/June* and *love/dove.*

CONCLUSION

This discussion of rhyme has covered millions of years, from the first mammalian isolation cry to the specific problems of English, a language that uses rhyme a great deal yet is rather impoverished in what can be made to rhyme. The vast canvas that I have painted, however sketchily, is probably more than most people would expect in a discussion of rhyme, but I hope I have shown that it is necessary. Certainly, dealing with English alone, I could have discussed nothing beyond the intricate aspects of what I have called *rhyme-2.* The more I thought about rhyme, however, and about phenomena close to it, such as alliteration, the more I felt: What can we know about rhyme if we only focus on rhyme, especially as the term itself is not precise and has an odd history? I have therefore rung the changes of the centuries, in an exercise that, I hope, puts rhyme in an ancient and profoundly significant context.

For rhyme is never alone. It rests on the rhythm of breath and speech, partnered and often blended with such other sound play as alliteration, assonance, consonance, onomatopoeia, repetition and parallelism. In turn, this playing with sound underpins and intermixes with playing with words and with rhetorical devices such as metaphor, simile and metonymy. The result may be as elegant as a sonnet or as street-smart as rap, but there is always something primordial about it, something so many thousands of years in the making that our children are born 'wired' for it and learn through it. They are far more like Mr Fox than Mr Knox, and are just as relentlessly in love with it all:

> *Mr. Fox!*
> *I hate this game, Sir.*
> *This game makes*
> *my tongue quite lame, sir.*
> *Mr. Knox, sir,*
> *That's a shame, sir.*
> *We'll find something*
> *new to do now.*
> *Here is lots of*
> *new blue goo now.*
> *New goo. Blue goo.*
> *Gooey. Gooey.*
> *Blue goo. New goo.*
> *Gluey. Gluey.*[1]

$\mathscr{R}$EFERENCES

1. From Seuss, Dr. G. (1960) *Fox in Socks: A Tongue Twister for Super Children.* New York: Randon House Inc.
2. For discussions of the paleontology of speech see: Leakey, R. and Lewin, R. (1992) *Origins Reconsidered: In Search of What Makes us Human.* Little, Brown and Company; Lieberman, P. (1991) *Uniquely Human: The Evolution of Speech, Thought and Selfless Behavior.* Harvard University Press; and Gibson, K.R. and Ingold, T. (eds) (1993) *Tools, Language and Cognition in Human Evolution.* Cambridge: Cambridge University Press
3. For a discussion of storage speech in the context of human communication, see the entry 'communicative shift' in McArthur, T. (ed) (1992) *The Oxford Companion to the English Language.* Oxford: Oxford University Press
4. For further information on rhythm, syllable-timing and stress-timing, etc., see: Abercrombie, D. (1967) *Elements of General Phonetics.* Edinburgh: Edinburgh University Press; Couper-Kuhlen, E. (1993) *English Speech Rhythm: Form and Function in Everyday Verbal Interaction.* Amsterdam and Philadelphia: John Benjamins; and the entries 'rhythm', 'stress' and 'syllable' in *The Oxford Companion* (above, Note 3).
5. For concise etymological statements on the words 'rhyme', 'rhythm' and 'rime' see *The Oxford English Dictionary* (second edition), 1989 for detail, and/or *The New Shorter Oxford English Dictionary*, 1993, for a more compact presentation of the same information.
6. From the entry 'rhyme', written jointly by Arthur Melville Clark and Harold Whitehall in Preminger, A. (ed.) (1974) *Princeton Encyclopedia of Poetry and Poetics.* London: Macmillan.
7. See note 3, above, for details of source.

3

❊❊❊❊❊❊❊❊❊❊❊❊❊❊❊❊❊❊❊❊❊❊❊❊❊❊❊❊❊❊❊❊❊❊❊❊❊❊

NONSENSE, RHYME AND WORD PLAY IN YOUNG CHILDREN

Marian Whitehead

> *'That's easy peasy,*
> *Lemon squeezy'*

This chirpy little rhyme was a six-year-old's response to his teacher's reprimand and her insistence that he complete the writing task she had set some time before. That it was a triumphant reaction which took all the sting out of the incident for the child was underlined by this next whispered comment to his friend, 'I'm used to being told off'.

I was visiting his classroom and this incident was a reminder to me of young children's delight in rhymes and their cheeky playfulness with words. It is an aspect of children's language which has intrigued and challenged parents and researchers for generations. There are several theories which try to explain why young children are so adept at playing with words and creating and remembering rhymes. This chapter aims to explore the power and charm of 'easy peasy' by looking at some aspects of nonsense and play with language in the early years (0–8 is the age range I have in mind).

NONSENSE AND LANGUAGE

> *'Have you got a sister?'*
> *'The beggarman kissed her!'*
> *'Have you got a brother?'*
> *'He's made of indiarubber!'*

> ·*'Have you got a baby?'*
> *'It's made of bread and gravy!'*

It is traditional rhymes like this[1] which may give us a clue to what makes children, and the adults they become, tick. The professional linguist can point out that the verse demonstrates questions and answers, exploits rhyming and chiming sound effects at the ends of the lines, and has the repeated pattern of 'Have you' at the start of every question. The psychologist will probably be able to identify some less obvious, but nonetheless powerful, themes concerned with family relationships and desperate jealousy; including a thinly disguised plot to get rid of a new baby rival by gobbling it up! For such consuming passions are just as prevalent in the nursery as in romantic 'soaps', novels and films. Students of childhood and culture will identify the ancient oral tradition of insults and teasing to which this rhyme belongs, and we can all agree that this little bit of nonsense is fun and easy to remember. The professional educator will probably go further and claim, as I do, that if we investigate this endearing kind of nonsense and play with language we are likely to find out more about childhood, language and the human mind.

A lively tradition of listening to very young children and recording their words and opinions already exists and the 'father' of this kind of research was Kornei Chukovsky, a Russian historian, critic, children's author and translator. In the 1920s he published a book[2] which demonstrated that children from two to five years of age are highly creative linguistic geniuses, tireless intellectual explorers and spontaneous poets. Modern research has reinforced all of Chukovsky's claims and it is easy to underestimate the impact of this revolutionary book which is crammed with stunning evidence of children's thinking and linguistic creativity. For example, he notes that young children do not learn language by simply imitating other people. On the contrary, they use what they know about grammatical rules and the world to which words refer to create expressions they cannot have overheard:

> *Three-year-old Nata:*
> *'Mommie, sing me a lullaby-ly song!'*[3]

Chukovsky claims that little children are tireless explorers of their social, physical and intellectual worlds and he shows how skilfully they use their limited information and experience, in combination with their impressive social skills, to ask just the right questions. The following exchange occurred after a very early exposure to the creation story according to Charles Darwin!

> *Nina asked her grandmother:*
> *'Granny, were you once a monkey?'*
> *'No, never.'*
> *'And your mother?'*
> *'Not either.'*
> *'Then who was a monkey? Grandpa?'*
> *'God be with you, child! No, grandpa not either.'*
> *'Oh, well, that means that my Moscow granny was the monkey.'* [4]

I am reminded at this point of the rigorous questioning of their parents by four-year-old girls in a study based in London in the early 1980s. [5] The topics of these 'grillings' ranged from the wages of window-cleaners to the construction of flat roofs. Like Nina, the London children did not so much require a final solution to their enquiries, as enough information to create a temporary resting place where they could mentally re-organise all that they knew, before setting out on the next stage of their investigations.

Chukovsky was aware of the futility of forcing adult solutions on children before they were able to understand them and make them part of their own thinking and experience. This view accounts for the long-lasting fame of his book, because it led to a chapter on nonsense verse which remains one of the best-known analyses of the significance of nonsense in childhood. But a little history is in order, for Chukovsky was writing in the newly created Soviet Russia of the years following the 1917 October Revolution. State ownership, atheism and socialist realism made an impact on child-rearing, as on everything else, including literature, particularly the folk literature of the oral tradition. So very young children were protected from fairy tales, nonsense and fantasy and exposed to Darwin, the physiological facts of conception and birth, and other 'socially useful information'. [6] However, Chukovsky provides clear evidence that little children still persevered in creating tall stories and nonsense out of the socially useful information forced on them.

This book draws our attention to young children's delight in violating the accepted notions of reality and turning conventional ideas upside down. It also asserts that children can only understand and create nonsense because they already have a well-developed grasp of 'sense'. Our oral traditions, such as nursery rhymes and folk and fairy tales, are full of the 'topsy-turvies'[7] which feed children's own experiments with their language and cultural traditions. After all, as Chukovsky reminds us, pre-Revolution Russian children would have been familiar with traditional stories of houses which ran around on chicken legs and people who galloped on all kinds of creatures except, of course, horses. Chukovsky describes this as the sense of nonsense because,

'With the help of fantasies, tall tales, fairy tales and topsy-turvies of every type, children confirm their realistic orientation to actuality.'[8]

In other words, the crazier the playful nonsense, the sounder the grasp of reality.

I was reminded of this on a recent visit to a Reception class where I heard the four- and five-year-olds enjoying a singsong during a wet playtime. Their favourite song which was repeated innumerable times was a chant consisting of the words,

'Kentucky Chicken, Pizza Hut, Happy Eater and McDonald's, McDonald's.'

This was accompanied by rhythmic clapping, finger-clicking, body-swaying and other actions, such as elbow-flapping for the chicken and circular movements for the pizza. What was very obvious was the strong social bond which this singing fostered in these little children in the early days of being a class. This apparently silly chant also highlighted the children's shared cultural experience: in this case, visits to fast food restaurants, another consuming passion in childhood. Traditional rhymes, songs and stories around the world are filled with references to food and the joys of eating, as well as the threat of being eaten. Furthermore, this love of talking about food is found among children's earliest 'first words' and phrases.[9]

The tradition pioneered by Chukovsky was developed in the UK by Iona and Peter Opie who observed children in streets and playgrounds for over forty years. (Their work is discussed further by Georgina Boyes in Chapter 8.) Like all good explorers and anthropologists the Opies brought back tales of a tribal culture rich in the language arts of song, dance, parody, taunt, vulgarity and subversion. These possibilities for play with language which the ancient tribe of children[10] exploits so successfully deserve closer investigation.

- Young children's delight in nonsense is an indicator of their understanding of reality.
- Attempts to by-pass this exploratory thinking by imposing adult information and realism too soon are misguided and ineffective.

PLAY AND LANGUAGE

A was an apple-pie;
B bit it,
C cut it,
D dealt it,
E eat it, ...
Traditional

Play and language are activities which are very similar in their use of symbols and metaphors. A symbol can be many things, including a word, a gesture, a toy, or even a uniform; such symbols stand for complex ideas, feelings, events or institutions. Think of what lies behind, and is symbolised by, a handshake, a religious ceremony, or a child's soft toy. Similarly, the use of metaphors helps us to refer to complicated matters by describing them briefly in terms of something that is instantly recognisable and memorable. We may talk of 'hitting the nail on the head' and save ourselves a lot of elaborate explanations. However, the metaphors have to be part and parcel (that is one) of a familiar and shared culture if they are to work. Languages and their accompanying gestures, their conventional phrases and the special 'registers' used for speaking to employers, lovers, doctors, infants and so on are not as straightforward and literal as we might like to think. The conventional language registers of the surgery, the classroom and the workplace are a kind of linguistic game we play, a game in which we borrow language and meanings from other settings. For example, we talk of 'fighting' disease and illiteracy, or 'nursing' a grievance. Layers of meanings and hints of stories attach themselves to phrases, gestures, expressions and the use of objects and clothes, so that adults and children are constantly escaping (another metaphor) the literal meanings of words. Even word definitions in dictionaries require column inches for the alternative meanings created by different contexts.

The multi-layered nature of language, and of play, makes it possible for us to deal with the complexities of our lives. Psychologists see language and play as essential to intelligent, adaptable behaviour. Richard Gregory, a professor of neuropsychology who studies the brain and its perceptions, links our passion for stories to the scientific method of creating hypotheses or theories. We use our stories about people and the world as theories for predicting likely outcomes and Gregory calls these kinds of stories 'brain fictions'.[11] All of us, adults and children alike, create scenarios for the future, tell tales of our past and use words and things to signal where we are, where we are coming from and where we may be going. From early infancy children play at being someone or something else and at being somewhere else; and they use different kinds of language, movement, facial expressions and objects to support these play scenarios. In these activities they are aided and abetted by their families, communities and cultures who share with them family reminiscences, old and new stories, sayings or songs, and also demonstrate certain behaviours and introduce them to rituals, traditions and figures of authority. This is all ideal material for young minds to work on: imitating, parodying, re-telling and turning it upside down. After all, if the simple ABC at the start of this section can be personified and turned into a tale of greed, desire, robbery and grief, the possibilities for exploiting the peculiarities of people are endless.

- Play and language use symbols and metaphors to stand for the complex, abstract and absent; be they ideas, feelings, objects or persons.

- Play and languages are aspects of intelligent behaviour. They work together to create stories which are theories about people and the world.

Playing a part

I'm the king of the castle,
You're the dirty rascal.

Playing a role is one of the most familiar of children's language and play activities known to parents, carers and early years teachers. Who has not come across young children wearing odd items of clothing and lengths of fabric, carrying props such as sticks, dolls or a 'magic' piece of paper, and announcing 'I'm a king', or 'I'm the Cookie Monster'? But imitating the roles played by others is not simple; it is a very sophisticated kind of acting, even in early childhood.

Firstly, it is highly selective and only certain crucial features of appearance, props, noises and language are picked on for imitation. These selected features act as symbols for the role: 'I'm a monster' usually involves lots of roaring, play-biting and gobbling of others. 'I'm a doctor' always requires 'the thing in my ears to listen to you'.

Secondly, role play is exaggerated; it has the 'over the top' quality of caricature. This is particularly evident when those in authority, usually parents and teachers, are the focus of the imitation. The concern with absolute power over others is very noticeable in young children's role play. All those not fortunate enough to be 'in charge' are beaten cruelly, sent to bed hungry, or given zero marks for their school work. This selection and exaggeration indicates an impressive grasp of the realities of people's roles in society and an understanding of how language works and is used differently in different contexts. Children's endless fascination with power and its misuse by authoritarian figures also hints at the vulnerability of childhood.

Role play may be embryonically present in the earliest social behaviours of babies. The evidence comes from researchers who have observed and recorded the skills of newborns who can imitate tongue-poking by an adult, lock their eye-gaze with their carer, and later copy smiling and laughter.[12] Eventually toddlers use their whole bodies to explore aspects of a new experience which has been exciting and even frightening. The psychologist Jean Piaget records finding his own daughter who was nearly four lying motionless on a sofa, 'her arms pressed against her body and her legs bent'.[13] On the previous day she had been impressed by her first sight of a duck which was on the kitchen table, plucked and trussed for the oven. Clearly she was trying out the experience of being an oven-ready duck and actually explained her posture by saying 'I'm the dead duck'. A more cheerful example of whole body role play is recorded by psychologist Susanna Millar who found her three-year-old son swinging his legs rhythmically from side to side: he was being a windscreen wiper.[14] In both these examples the children are using their bodies in a kind of role play which investigates some emotional and physical aspects of their worlds; they are literally learning through playing a role.

When children find objects in their environment which they then use as props in their role play, they are at the start of a major intellectual achievement. Lev Vygotsky, the Russian psychologist and linguist who was writing in the 1930s, drew attention to the significance of 'pivots'[15] which mark the beginnings of symbolic play, symbolic language use and representational thinking. This is a cluster of very complex ideas which actually attempts to explain the nature of human thinking, so we cannot expect it to be easy. For the purposes of this discussion, we can accept that one of the most powerful features of human thinking and language is our ability to talk about and think about objects, ideas and people which are not in front of us, or have never existed, or cannot be explained easily. These are the very situations for which we need the symbols and metaphors discussed earlier and children's choices of props or pivots for role play indicate the start of their ability to separate mentally the meanings of words from objects in the world. For example, in young children's play wine corks can be 'sausages' and a rolled cloth can be a 'dolly'. The example developed by Vygotsky is a young child's use of a stick as a 'horse'; the stick is treated 'as if' it were a horse because it is possible to gallop along with it between the legs, rein it in and dismount. It is already a kind of metaphor because it has been named 'horse', although the child also knows that it is a stick. A temporary ignoring of the literal reality of sticks allows the child to concentrate on the 'horsey' things about this particular stick: its gallop-able, straddle-able qualities.

So here we have a remarkable feature of human thinking already established in the pre-school years: words can be divorced from the things they usually refer to, and things can be described with words that literally mean something else. Digging a flower 'bed', or leaving the car in a 'park' without swings or ducks are unremarkable activities, but as linguistic references they may reflect the existence in the mind of areas of overlap where 'car' and 'park' can co-exist and enrich our thinking. Perhaps role play is the crucial intellectual activity which underpins all the issues raised by this chapter and even by this book. Playing with language, exploring meanings and subverting what we know, are all roles which children and adults take up readily.

- Playing a role occurs early in children's development and may originate in their first social responses as babies.
- Role play is not simple imitation, it is highly selective and exaggerated.
- In role play children use symbolic props; this indicates their ability to think by representing ideas, feelings, etc., with words and objects.

EXPLORING MEANINGS

> *I'll tell you a story*
> *about Jack a Nory,*
> *And now my story's begun...*
> Traditional

Telling a story, remembering the past, or speculating about the future, are all aspects of the human tendency to think in narrative.[16] This is a key way in which we make sense of experience and cope with our lives. Educators describe narrative as a crucial feature of children's thinking and Gordon Wells has described the children he studied for ten years, from infancy through primary school, as 'the meaning makers'.[17] Mention has already been made of stories as theories about life and we have already noted the rich resources of traditional tales, beliefs and rhymes which exist to be tapped into, in every culture. When children try to understand something they often inadvertently create a bizarre or amusing story, as with these Reception class children watching their captive snails:

> *Sarah* 'Look at the little snail and there's his big mum in the grass.'
>
> *David* 'I can see all the slimy on the glass.'
>
> *Kevin* 'Is it like glue? Not glue like when we do sticking at school.'
>
> *Sarah* 'Not that white sort of glue, like ...'
>
> *Richard* 'I did sticking, I made a big card for my Nan.'[18]

These children appear to exploit every scrap of their experiences both inside and outside school, to make links between the things they do know and the strange things happening in front of their eyes. Furthermore, the power of family relationships to hold their world together comes through: little snails need big mums and the important thing about doing sticking at school is making a card for Nan.

The humour here is incidental and a reflection of the children's limited experience of the world, but the work of Chukovsky reminds us that nonsense is such an important meaning-making tool, part of the serious business of childhood, that children constantly invent their own special nonsense.

Children's play with the meanings of words is often a source of spontaneous humour and delight; as they try to find out the meanings of words they alert us to the poetry and the incongruity which pervades our everyday use of language. I like to think of this as the 'wow' factor in children's language development. It is certainly an experience familiar to parents, carers and teachers of young children and a recent example I encountered is fairly typical.

The scene is a hotel swimming pool on a hot summer day. A very confident three-year-old has been playing in and around the pool for some days with a group of kindly eight- and nine-year-old boys. On this particular day one of the older boys is called away by his parents and the reason given to the group is that he is going on a trip. The effect on the three-year-old is extraordinary. He becomes convulsed with laughter and staggers around the edge of the pool, elaborately pretending to trip over the paving, while shouting constantly, 'He's going on a trip today!' His mirth is quite infectious and soon the older boys are giggling and extending the joke by asking the little one, in chorus, 'Is he going on a trip today?', thus reducing him to near-hysterical repetitions of his performance. Clearly he was discovering a new meaning of the word 'trip' and finding it a huge joke. Furthermore, his public comic turn reminded me of that old and slightly heartless response used when someone does trip over: 'Had a nice trip?' Children's jokes are often based on word play of this kind, but they can also be the 'topsy-turvies' discussed earlier, when actuality and ideas about the world are subverted, taboos are broken and a little mayhem rules.

- Children make sense of the world by creating stories and nonsensical accounts.
- Children explore the meanings of words and language in playful ways.
- Language is not just a system for communicating and transmitting information; children's play with words and meanings must be nurtured and valued.

SUBVERTING THE SYSTEM

> *Neighbours,*
> *Pick your nose and taste the flavours.*
>
> South-east London, 1994

> *Neighbours*
> *Vanilla, Strawberry and Quavers.*
>
> Edinburgh, 1994

We are probably all familiar with this kind of subverting of popular songs, media theme tunes, hymns, carols, poems and advertising jingles. These two contemporary examples are typical in that one relies on naming a publicly unacceptable personal habit, thus violating a minor taboo, and the other plays about with the conventions of advertising copy. But this subversion is not the trivial activity it appears to be and some serious points can be made about the drive, apparent in early childhood and through to adolescence, and even beyond, to subvert the systems of language and culture.

Firstly, as this chapter has already indicated, one of the best ways of getting to understand something is to take it apart and then re-assemble it, often with additions and changes which make it your own. This applies to children's early language learning, as in their experiments with past tenses (I goed), with plurals (mouses) and with word meanings,

'I'm not a grasshopper! I'm a people'[19]

It is reflected in their role play and in their play with objects and materials, as any carer who has had a VCR or the remote control unit deconstructed will know. When children and adults do similar things with the literature, beliefs, traditions, rules and assumptions of their cultures it is challenging and subversive. As a method of understanding serious literature and its relationship to society, subversion has now become academically respectable and is usually labelled 'carnival'.[20] The notion of carnival is useful because it relates to that deep instinct to resist control and uniformity which is so apparent in children's rude or silly versions of rhymes and other registers of language. Furthermore, it reminds us that any text, no matter how serious, can be questioned, manipulated and re-worked. Carnival always involves elements of parody, role-reversal ('queen for a day'), rudeness, sexual licence, boisterous humour and a general sense of time-off from good behaviour and conformity.[21] The 'easy peasy' at the head of this chapter is an example of a carnivalesque response by a young dissident to a teacher's reprimand and it highlights two other aspects of subversion. Carnival has always been tolerated because it provides a safety valve for the potentially subversive elements in any system or social group, but carnival can also lead to a permanent shift in power and attitudes.

The safety valve aspect of carnival may mean just one or two days of relaxation and 'changing places' in a year; whether it be permission to abandon school uniform one day a term, a birthday party binge on jelly and crisps, or a media-sponsored spending spree for one lucky competition winner. At this level subversion is easily tolerated because it does little to upset the 'status quo' and actually works to strengthen it by letting off a little steam in a harmless kind of way.

But whenever carnival occurs things can, and do, get out of hand. A little subversion is rarely the straightforward safety valve that it appears to be, and entrenched views and policies have been changed by the power of cartoons, satires and parodies. The subversive material and behaviour loved by children and adults too can also help to defuse pain, terror and powerlessness. No one needs this kind of help more than small vulnerable children who do not know what is really going on in a world they cannot control, as 'easy peasy' indicates. This defusing is clearly going on when children either appear to be pushing the boundaries of behaviour in order to find out 'How far can I go?' or, when they are probing the power of adults to find 'How far can they go?' When the child is testing 'How far can I go?', the breaking of taboos about referring to bodily functions and sexual activities is a common symptom, as playground researchers soon discover. The material collected by Iona Opie from a primary school playground[22] has a vulgarity and an energy which reduces me to mealy-mouthed censorship. However, the recurring themes recorded by Opie of sexual curiosity, plus parodies of teachers, lessons and school routines, along with the predictable attacks on the horrors of school dinners, confirm the significance of boundary testing in childhood. (Georgina Boyes refers to other instances in Chapter 8.)

When children are probing the extent of adult power the themes are often violent, or they have the cruel slap-stick quality found in comics. We have already noted the ways in which little children role-play disturbingly punitive mums, dads, teachers and, in one instance recorded by Carol Fox and her colleagues, a 'doctor' whose prescription for an ailing baby doll was, 'Let's bash her in the face'[23]! The need to explore in play just how dangerous the all-powerful adults might be and, by working through a few worst-case scenarios, defuse some of the unspeakable anxiety, is paralleled in the literature of childhood. In the nursery rhymes tongues are slit, old men are thrown down the stairs and children are whipped. In the fairy tales children are abandoned, eyes are put out and the innocent suffer terrible transformations into beasts. Contemporary children's literature also has its dark woods, unhappy children, fierce monsters and apocalyptic visions of a grim future.

Clearly this desire to frighten ourselves is not new and it is not even limited to childhood, for adults also like to expose themselves to controlled amounts of fear. There is interesting evidence from psychology and anthropology that we gain control over our fears by pushing ourselves and our infants to the 'edge of terror'.[24] Just think of all those games with babies when we throw them in the air, pretend almost to drop them, and play at 'peep-boo'. And what about 'hide-and-seek' in dark cupboards and under furniture? Adults and adolescents frequently participate in activities which frighten them, or have a high risk factor, and these strange behaviours have been found in many different cultures. The anthropologist Clifford Geertz calls them 'deep play', mainly because of the degree of risk and terror involved and the attraction they appear to hold for the players who voluntarily put themselves through a variety of ordeals.[25] The kind of literature which has a similar hold on children provides all the terror of deep play, but it also offers the safety net of language which contains and comfortably distances the experience. The function of language is to name the unspeakable fear and give it a manageable identity.[26] So Max meets his Wild Things, rampages with them, and then controls them with the magical words of control, 'Now Stop!'. The myths of many cultures have evolved to enable all of us to 'manage our monsters'[27] and turn them into stories which might end happily ever after, although it is often a close run thing. The darker play themes of childhood have their share of fear, pain, taboo and the wickedest words we can utter, but rhyme, poetry and song contain and soothe the pain within a rhythmic and pleasing pattern.

- Subversion is a way of understanding which involves taking apart and re-assembling. Children frequently use this learning strategy with new words, ideas and objects.
- Carnival is a traditional kind of subversion which challenges social control and conventions.
- Children's carnivalesque play explores possibilities and defuses deep anxieties.

Rhyme and poetic language

> *'Way*
> *Far*
> *Now*
> *It a church bell*
> *Ringin'*
> *Dey singing*
>   *ringin'*
> *You hear it?*
> *I hear it*
> *Far*
> *Now'* [28]

Two-and-a-half-year-old Lem created this poem-like story in response to the sound of a bell which must have reminded him of his visit to church on the previous Sunday. He does not simply tell us how much he enjoyed the singing, rocking and hand-clapping of the black community church he had been taken to, he actually re-makes a version of that experience. So this little 'poem' has repetition, rhyme and the rhythmic pattern of ritual questions and answers. It is a remarkable achievement for a two-year-old, even one living in an isolated community with a strong oral culture. Lem's story about church can be called a poem because it has several features of poetic language, including rhyme, and the tender age of the poet suggests that these features may develop early in childhood, long before organised schooling has any influence. So we are back to looking at language development in families and communities again.

Any exploration of rhyme in early childhood must begin with a basic definition of the concept; so, if 'easy peasy' is rhyme, what is rhyme? Rhyme is matching or identical sounds in words or in the end sounds of lines of verse (what Tom McArthur calls 'Rhyme-2' in Chapter 2): 'easy' and 'peasy' are word rhymes and a rhyming verse is,

> *Boys and girls come out to play,*
> *The moon does shine as bright as day.*
>
>   Traditional

Rhyme is an effect produced by the sounds of a language and sound is the very substance of language itself, as the previous chapter has explained. This emphasis on sound brings us back to the beginnings of language in every child and the physical nature of its production. The sounds of language are shaped in the mouth, as an outgoing stream of air from the lungs passes through and between soft and hard palate, nasal cavity, tongue, gums, teeth and lips. This physical experience is very noticeable when small babies and toddlers try to speak and communicate; their bodies bounce with excitement and arms and legs move rhythmically with the mouth sounds. Physical pleasure in making sounds is bound up with language development from the start. We can see further evidence of this in the young baby's early language practice with mouth sounds, commonly known as babbling. The importance of this for understanding rhyme is that much of the pleasure of babbling arises from the physical sensation of repeating the same sounds in the same parts of the mouth over and over again. This pleasure and ease of articulation still satisfies us long after we are not expected to babble. Think about singing a tune with 'la-la-la' in place of words, the jazz singer's scat, or rhythmic repetitive chants at football matches, demonstrations and political rallies: 'easy, easy, easy', for example. Simple one-word chants are repeated patterns of articulation in the same areas of the mouth, as are tongue-twisters, raps and taunts such as 'Cowardy, cowardy, custard'.

This latter taunt is a reminder of some related aspects of poetic language. Just as rhyme focuses our attention on end sounds, so the beginnings of words can have identical or similar sounds which we call alliteration: 'Peter Piper picked a peck of pickled peppers'.

Words and phrases can also be repeated again and again with dramatic effect. Small children enjoy this latter effect as much as professional poets do and most parents and early years professionals can recall delightful examples of a new word, or phrase, repeated endlessly and for sheer pleasure. Regular routines and rituals in infancy and childhood tend to acquire these easy, rhyming, verse snippets which comfort and reassure, although their folk origins may be in a harsher world: 'Goodnight, sleep tight, make sure the bugs don't bite!'

All this suggests that the raw material of poetry is present in children's earliest language learning. What is so fresh and striking to the young child about the sounds of a language, the rhythmic patterns of words, the endless possibilities for repeating and re-ordering them, is the essence of literary language and the basis of literacy. This early sensitivity to the poetic material of language has important implications for children's literacy development and will be developed in other contributions to this volume. But it is significant that linguists now study the ways in which language is used in works of literature. They look at rhyme, repetition, alliteration and other patterns with words, rhythms and sounds, and at least one researcher has started from a discussion of nursery rhymes.[29] Much of this research material is highly technical and I would summarise it as a way of demonstrating that poetic language, whether it be Lem's celebration of church or Dylan Thomas's lament for his dying father[30], draws attention to itself as language. It is not just 'what' is said that matters, the 'way' of saying it is an essential part of the message, and often *is* the message. This concern with particular words in a particular order has the effect of arresting our attention, so that we attend to words and meanings in an especially close way.

I would not wish to suggest that poetic language is all material and no matter; much of my earlier discussion of nonsense indicated the powerful meanings carried by apparently daft behaviour, tall stories and nonsensical verses. But the effect of rhyme, choice of words, and repetition, is to slow down our reading and responses. So much so that even the youngest child can remember, hold on to, own and think about abstract ideas like 'up' and 'down', for example:

> *And when they were up, they were up,*
> *And when they were down, they were down,*
> *And when they were only half-way up,*
> *They were neither up nor down.*
>
> The brave old Duke of York, traditional

Lots of repetition, lots of pleasing rhymes and lots of amusing, sad or puzzling ideas help children to remember language and investigate it. We have research evidence which shows that little children alone in bed will go over the events and the language of their day; they practise saying new words and phrases (rather like repetitive foreign language exercises) and babble strings of words and nonsense syllables which rhyme or start with identical sounds.[31] These games with words and sounds also trigger reflections about recent events and the people who care for them. Perhaps here we can find not just the material of poetic play with language, but also the matter of poetry. By this I mean poetry's ability to preserve the essential feel of experience; its concern to celebrate life and its role in mourning our losses. A little ambitious for early childhood perhaps? Well, not if we look at the work of gifted teachers and carers who have nurtured children's taste for language from the crib, the family, and the playground and into the classroom.

- Rhyme is a sound effect of language and has links with infants' early explorations of mouth sounds.
- Repetition of same and similar sounds is part of the poetic aspect of a language, as are rhythms and other patterned forms of language.
- Poetic language exploits pleasurable sounds and draws our attention to linguistic forms and meanings.
- Poetry, nursery rhymes, nonsense verse, tongue-twisters, music and dance should be central features of an appropriate early years curriculum, as should talking and listening.

CONCLUSION

In the previous chapter, Tom McArthur found it necessary to cover centuries of linguistic history in order to provide an account of the nature of rhyme. Similarly, my own attempt to explore nonsense, rhyme and word play in young children seems to have taken us all round the houses and down the by-ways of play, representation and subversion. In the process I have succeeded in convincing myself of the truth of Tom McArthur's claim that children are probably 'wired' for rhyme and language play and are 'relentlessly in love with it all'.

But the questions usually asked of an early years educator at the end of this kind of exercise are, 'Can this be taught?, or, 'What implications does this have for carers and educators?'.

My answer to both questions is that infants' wiring and their capacity for a lifelong love affair with language still require the right connections to be made with the power of a culture and its ways of using language. Just as we talk to our babies and treat them as potential speakers from birth, so we also need to share with them that inner rhymer and poet responsible for our own daily linguistic play. Because we too play with the sound and the sense of language in every metaphor we use and in all our slips of the tongue, our jokes, our songs and our awareness of amusing names and unintended rhymes. 'I'm a poet and don't know it' we may have said in our own childhood, but as adults who care for and educate young children we must claim a conscious responsibility for nurturing rhyme and word play; our own and theirs. After all, the power and the pleasure of nonsense, rhyme and alliterative play with language may also be the key to literacy.

*R*EFERENCES

1. Opie, I., Opie, P. (eds.) and Sendak, M. (1992) I Saw Esau, in *The Schoolchild's Pocket Book*, London: Walker
2. Chukovsky, K. (1963) *From Two to Five*, Berkeley: University of California Press
3. Chukovsky, p.4
4. Chukovsky, p.41
5. Tizard, B. and Hughes, M. (1984) *Young Children Learning*, London: Fontana
6. Chukovsky, K. (1963) *From Two to Five*, Berkeley: University of California Press
7. Chukovsky, p.94
8. Chukovsky, p.113
9. Engel, D.M. and Whitehead, M.R. (1993) 'More First Words' in *Early Years*, 14, 1, pp.27–35
10. Lurie, A. (1990) Don't Tell the Grown-Ups in *Subversive Children's Literature*, London: Bloomsbury
11. Gregory, R.L. (1977) 'Psychology: towards a science of fiction' in Meek, M., Warlow, A. and Barton, G. (eds), *The Cool Web*, London: Bodley Head p.394
12. Trevarthen, C. (1993) 'Playing into Reality' in *Winnicott Studies*, 7, pp.67–84

13. Piaget, J. (1951) *Play, Dreams and Imitation in Childhood*, London: Routledge and Kegan Paul, p.133

14. Millar, S. (1968) *The Psychology of Play*, Harmondsworth: Penguin p.146

15. Vygotsky, L.S. (1978) *Mind in Society*, Cambridge, Mass.: Harvard University Press p.97

16. Hardy, B. (1977) 'Towards a poetics of fiction: an approach through narrative' in Meek, M. Warlow, A. and Barton, G. (eds), *The Cool Web*, London: Bodley Head pp.12–23

17. Wells, G. (1987) *The Meaning Makers*, London: Hodder and Stoughton

18. Hughes, M. (1994) 'The Oral Language of Young Children' in Wray, D. and Medwell, J. (eds.) *Teaching Primary English*, London: Routledge p.19

19. Chukovsky, K. (1963) *From Two to Five*, Berkeley: University of California Press p.5

20. Bakhtin, M. (1968) *Rabelais and his World*, Cambridge, Mass.: Harvard University Press

21. Whitehead, M.R. (1993) 'Born Again Phonics and the Nursery Rhyme Revival' in *English in Education*, 27, 3, pp.42–51

22. Opie, I. (1993) *The People in the Playground*, Oxford: Oxford University Press

23. Fox, *et al.* (1994) 'Genres, Anti-genres and the Art of Subversion in Children's Stories and Play' in *English in Education*, 28, 2, p.20

24. Bruner, J.S. (1976) 'Nature and Uses of Immaturity' in Bruner, J.S., Jolly, A. and Sylva, K. (eds.) *Play: Its Role in Development and Evolution*, Harmondsworth: Penguin, p.48

25. Geertz, C. (1976) 'Deep Play: a description of the Balinese cockfight' in Bruner, *et al.*, (eds.) *Play*, pp. 656–74

26. Sendak, M. (1967) *Where the Wild Things Are*, London: Bodley Heath

27. Warner, M. (1994) *Managing Monsters*, The 1994 Reith Lectures, London: Vintage

28. Heath, S.B. (1983) *Ways with Words*, Cambridge; Cambridge University Press p.170

29. Hasan, R. (1989) *Linguistics, Language and Verbal Art*, Oxford: Oxford University Press

30. Thomas, D. (1952)'Do not Go Gentle Into That Good Night' in *Collected Poems 1934–1952*, London: Dent p.159

31. Weir, R.H. (1962) *Language in the Crib*, The Hague: Mouton

RHYME IN CHILDREN'S EARLY READING

Usha Goswami

> *My brothers read a little bit – little words like* if *and* it.
> *My Father can read big words, too, like* Constantinople *and* Timbuktu.

Rhyme is an important part of childhood. Children's pleasure in nursery rhymes and singing games has long been observed and documented[1], and the modern child's knowledge of advertising jingles and pop songs demonstrates that children's love of rhyme is as widespread as ever. Most nursery schools incorporate rhyme and song into their everyday activities, using songs not only to teach rhythm and rhyme, but also to teach other skills such as number (via counting rhymes). This focus on rhyme is very fortunate, as experimental studies have demonstrated a strong and specific connection between early rhyming and later reading development. In this chapter, we will look at some of the evidence for the connection between rhyme and reading, and assess some of the practical implications of the findings of research studies for teaching reading in the classroom.

THE DEVELOPMENT OF RHYME AWARENESS

The first step in discovering when children become aware of rhyme is to look at their language development and see when they begin to use rhymes spontaneously. In fact, most children go through a period of enjoying and inventing rhymes when they are between 2 and 3 years of age. A Russian study by

Kornei Chukovsky (which Roger Beard and Marian Whitehead also refer to in their chapters) documented the spontaneous invention of rhymes in children as young as 18 months: 'Endlessly he jabbers rhymed nonsense; for hours he "talks" to himself in rhymed syllables: alia, valia, dalia, malia'.[2] Chukovsky described young children as 'avid creators of word rhythms and rhymes' and reproduced some of their invented poems. Here is Tania's poem about milk:

> *Ilk-silk-tilk*
> *I eat Kasha with milk*
> *Ilks-silks-tilks*
> *I eat Kashas with milks.*

Tania, who was three-and-a-half, made up nonsense words like 'tilks'to suit her poem. This spontaneous invention of rhyming words to fit made-up poems has been documented in English children, too, by Ann Dowker[3], whose children made rhymes like:

> *The bird does jump,*
> *Mump and dump.*

However, it is interesting to note that many popular English nursery rhymes actually provide rather few demonstrations of proper rhymes. 'Baa Baa Black Sheep', for example, rhymes 'dame' with 'lane', and 'Old Mother Hubbard' rhymes 'bone' with 'none'. 'Little Tommy Tucker' rhymes 'supper' with 'butter', and 'Goosey, Goosey Gander' rhymes 'gander' with 'wander'.

A more formal way of investigating the development of rhyme is to ask children to tell you whether one word rhymes with another. In an early study of this kind[4], children were asked to decide which of two words rhymed with a third. For example, the target word might be 'pear', and the children were asked to say which word rhymed with 'pear', 'chair' or 'flag'. The experimenters found that most 4-year-old children had little difficulty in this task.

A different way of asking the same question is to ask children to choose the 'odd word out' of a set of words that rhyme. Lynette Bradley and Peter Bryant used this 'oddity' task with a large group of 4- and 5-year-old children in Oxford.[5] The children had to choose the odd word out of sets of words like 'pin', 'bun', 'gun'. Bradley and Bryant found that even the youngest children in their study managed this task extremely well. The rhyme task was also easier than a version of the oddity task based on alliteration ('hill', 'pig', 'pin').

Both anecdotal and research evidence thus shows that rhyming ability is present in preschool children, and that children can solve rhyme detection tasks by at least 4 years of age. More recent investigations of the development of rhyme have focused on the degree of *phonemic similarity* between rhyming words and their distractors. A phoneme is the smallest unit of sound that changes the meaning of a word. 'Pear' and 'chair' differ by a single phoneme, sharing the majority of their phonemes, and so do 'pin' and 'win'. 'Pin' and 'sit' only share a single phoneme, the sound of the vowel, and 'pear' and 'flag' have no shared phoneme. This *phonemic* analysis predicts that it might be cognitively simpler for a child to recognise that 'pear' and 'flag' do not rhyme than to recognise that 'flan' and 'flag' do not rhyme, as the former pair of words do not share any phonemes. Recognising that 'flag' and 'flan' do not rhyme might be more difficult, as these two words share all of their phonemes except one.

Margaret Snowling and her colleagues have shown that the degree of phonemic similarity between words indeed affects children's ability to make judgements about shared rhymes.[6] For example, it is more difficult to pick the odd word out in the triple 'job', 'rob', 'nod' than in the triple 'job', 'rob', 'knock', as 'd' (-od) is phonemically closer to 'b' (-ob) than 'k' (ock). The fact that children are sensitive to these fine phonemic contrasts suggests that recognising rhymes can help to develop a child's awareness of phonemes. It also suggests an interesting possibility about the learning experiences provided by nursery rhymes like Baa Baa Black Sheep. It might actually be very useful for children to have to listen closely to 'near miss' rhymes like 'dame' and 'lane' (what Tom McArthur refers to as 'assonance' or examples of 'Rhyme-1') *as well as* to gain experience with proper rhymes like 'wool' and 'full', as the 'non-rhymes' provide informal instruction in phonemic contrasts. Although this possibility has received no research attention, it does suggest that teachers could actually make a teaching point out of which pairs of words in nursery rhymes do and do not rhyme.

THE LINK BETWEEN RHYME AWARENESS AND LEARNING TO READ

Longitudinal Studies

In order to discover whether early rhyming skill is related to later reading development, we need to follow children over a period of time. We need to know whether rhyming ability measured at Time 1, before the children go to school, is related to reading ability at Time 2, when the children are learning to read. Reading ability in such 'longitudinal' studies is usually measured after two or more years at school, so that the children have had sufficient instruction in reading to enable individual differences to emerge.

One of the most comprehensive research studies of this kind was the longitudinal study by Bradley and Bryant[5], part of which has already been mentioned. They gave around 400 children in Oxfordshire the oddity rhyme task when they were 4 and 5 years of age, and followed up 368 of them three to four years later, measuring their progress in reading and spelling when the children were 8 and 9 years old. They found a strong *predictive* relationship between early rhyming and later reading. Children with good initial rhyming skills tended to become better readers and spellers, and this relationship held even after other variables, including IQ, vocabulary and memory, were taken into account. The relationship with rhyme was also specific to reading: no predictive relationship was found between rhyming ability and progress in mathematics. Hence the connection between rhyme and learning to read does not simply reflect general cognitive ability. Other longitudinal studies of the relationship between rhyme and reading, including studies carried out in other countries, have generally found similar results to those reported by Bradley and Bryant[5].

Studies of Backward Readers

A different way of investigating the same question is to look at the rhyming skills of backward readers. This can also help us to decide whether there is a causal connection between rhyming ability and reading progress. If the development of rhyming skill is an important predictor of the efficiency of reading acquisition, then children who have failed to acquire reading efficiently might be expected to have poor rhyming skills. However, the important thing here is the comparison group. If the rhyming skills of backward readers are compared to those of children of their own age, then the relationship between reading and rhyming is wholly ambiguous. A study comparing 10-year-old poor readers with 10-year-old good readers which found that the poorer readers were also poorer rhymers would tell us very little about the direction of the cause–effect relationship between rhyming and reading. The poor reading skills of the poor readers could be the cause of their poor rhyming skills, rather than vice versa. However, if the rhyming skills of the 10-year-old poor readers were compared to those of younger children reading at the same level as them (the 'reading level match design') and a rhyming deficit was still found, then this deficit would be better evidence for a causal connection between rhyming and reading.

In fact, a number of studies using the reading level match have demonstrated that backward readers do show significant deficits in rhyming tasks when compared to younger controls. For example, Bradley and Bryant gave their oddity task to a group of 10-year-old backward readers, and compared their performance to that of a group of 7-year-old children matched for reading level.[8] The older children made significantly more errors in the rhyming task than the younger children, and they also had more difficulty in thinking of words to rhyme with simple target words like 'dog' and 'boat'. The demonstration that backward readers have poorer rhyming skills than those of children who are much younger than they are provides further evidence that rhyming is connected to reading.

THE ROLE OF ANALOGIES IN LINKING READING AND RHYMING

One obvious question that follows from all of this research is why there should be a connection between rhyming and reading at all. After all, the English spelling system is based on the alphabet. Single alphabetic letters do not correspond to rhymes. Instead, most alphabet letters represent single *phonemes*. The letter 'd' represents the sound at the beginning of 'dog' and at the end of 'had', the letter 't' represents the sound at the beginning of 'toy' and at the end of 'cat', and so on. Rhymes tend to correspond to *groups* of alphabetic letters. The rhyme in 'cat' and 'hat' is represented by the letters 'at', the rhyme in 'ball' and 'wall' is represented by the letters 'all', and the rhyme in 'card' and 'hard' is represented by the letters 'ard'. At first glance, then, learning to read seems to have very little to do with rhyme. It seems to have much more to do with trying to decipher strings of alphabet letters.

However, consider the task facing the young child trying to decipher the strings of letters representing 'cat', 'ball' and 'card'. The sound made by the vowel 'a' in each of these words is totally different. If fact, most of the vowel sounds in English are highly ambiguous. The variability of vowel pronunciations are only reduced when the consonants that follow the vowel are taken into account. The 'a' sound in '-at' is always consistent with its sound in 'cat' and the 'a' sound in '-ard' is always consistent with its sound in 'card'. Margaret Stanback has demonstrated that the 17,602 words in the Carroll, Davis and Richman (1971) word frequency corpus for children are made up of only 824 different rimes, 616 of which recur in word 'families'.[9] In an early analysis of the 500 most frequently used words in primary reading books, it was shown that knowledge of only 37 rimes was sufficient to read all of them.[10] This gives us a clue about the importance of rhyme for reading development in English. A focus on rhyme can significantly *reduce* the difficulty of the learning task for beginning readers, as the correspondence between the spelling sequences that represent rhymes and their sounds in spoken words is far more consistent than the correspondence between single alphabet letters and individual phonemes.

Linguists call the unit that reflects the rhyming sound in two words the *rime.*[11] In this chapter, the term *rime* will be used as a shorthand for referring to the spelling sequences in different words that reflect the rhyming sound, such as '-at', '-all' and '-ard'. Evidence that young children do take account of rime-level information early in learning to read has come from studies of the *analogies* that children make between the shared spelling patterns in different words. An 'analogy' in reading depends on using the spelling-sound information in one word, such as 'light', to read a new word that shares the same spelling pattern, such as 'fight'. An analogy from 'light' to 'fight' depends on rhyme. A child who realises that 'light' can be used as a *clue* for reading 'fight' is making the prediction that the new word ('fight') will rhyme with the known word ('light') because it shares the spelling pattern for the rime.

Studies of reading analogies in young children have shown that analogies based on rimes are used before analogies based on other shared spelling units in words.[12,13] The experimental technique in these studies was to teach children to read one word, a 'clue' word such as 'beak', and then to give them new words to read that shared different portions of the spelling pattern with 'beak'. For example, words like 'peak' and 'weak' shared the rime with 'beak', and words like 'bean' and 'bead' shared the initial spelling unit ('bea-'). These *clue word* studies showed that rime analogies ('beak'–'peak') were used from the very beginning of reading by 5- and 6-year-old children. Other kinds of analogy, such as 'beginning' analogies, that depended on shared initial letter sequences ('beak'–'bean') emerged somewhat later.[14,15] Thus analogies based on shared rimes emerge *first* in reading development.

INDIVIDUAL DIFFERENCES IN CHILDREN'S USE OF RIME ANALOGIES

Another interesting finding to emerge from these clue word analogy studies was that some children used more rime analogies than others. When the factors underlying these individual differences were examined, it was found that children's use of rime analogies was closely correlated to their level of *rhyming* skill. Children with good rhyming skills used lots of analogies, and children with poorer rhyming skills did not. For example, in one study[16], children were given Bradley and Bryant's oddity task as a measure of rhyme awareness, and a consonant deletion task as a measure of phoneme awareness (consonant deletion requires the children to remove either the first sound ['beak'–'eak'] or the final sound ['beak–'bea'] from a single-syllable word).[17] This study found that, whereas individual variation in rhyming skill was intimately connected to individual variation in the use of rime analogies, individual variation in consonant deletion skill was not. The connection between rime analogies and rhyme thus seems to be a highly specific one.[18]

If differences in children's rhyming skills partly explain differences in their use of rime analogies, then a clear prediction follows. Children with markedly poor rhyming skills, such as children who are having difficulty in learning to read, should not show much spontaneous use of rime analogies. As their rhyming skills are relatively weak, they should lack the phonological foundation necessary to make predictions about the rhyming sounds of new words on the basis of shared spelling patterns with known words.

Studies carried out in Canada have confirmed that children with reading difficulties show little spontaneous use of rime analogies. For example, Maureen Lovett and her colleagues taught a group of 8-year-old dyslexic children to recognise some simple monosyllabic words, such as 'weak' and 'part'.[19] The children were then given new words, such as 'peak' and 'cart', to try and read. Even though they could reliably remember how to read 'weak' and 'part', the dyslexic children were unable to read the new words, despite the possibility of using rime analogies. Although the first set of words did not remain visibly present, thus making this study rather different from the studies using the 'clue word' technique, the children's almost complete inability to make a connection between the first set of words and the second seems remarkable. Much younger normally reading children *are* able to make such connections, even when clue words are no longer available.[20]

A CAUSAL-DEVELOPMENTAL MODEL OF LEARNING TO READ

The research studies described above can be simply summarised. Firstly, there is a strong and robust connection between rhyming and reading. Secondly, children with good rhyming skills make more rime analogies than children with weaker rhyming skills, and children with extremely poor rhyming skills do not seem to make rime analogies at all. As individual differences in rhyming skill predict individual differences in reading progress, it is tempting to conclude that individual differences in children's use of rime analogies play a role in explaining this relationship. Peter Bryant and I put forward a model of the relationship between phonological skills and learning to read that tried to capture this connection between rime analogies and progress in reading.[21] A version of our model is produced in Figure 4.1.

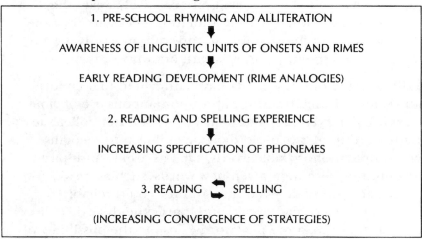

FIGURE 4.1. *A causal-developmental theory of reading*

As the model shows, early phonological knowledge about rhymes is thought to feed into early reading via the use of rime analogies. As children gain reading experience, and particularly as they learn to spell, reading progress comes to depend on *phonemic* knowledge. The relationship between individual alphabet letters and individual sounds is very important for *writing* words, and it is at this point in development that most children seem to begin to understand fully the concept of a phoneme.[22] It is worth pointing out, however, that our model is not intended to provide a *complete* explanation of reading development. It is a model about one set of causal factors that are related to reading, namely, phonological skills, and it is intended to show that phonological skills at different levels may contribute to reading development at different times.

Of course, children may also be explicitly *taught* the connections between individual alphabet letters and individual sounds (which is *not* the same thing as teaching phonemic awareness), and our model is quite neutral about when this teaching should occur. Opinion about the importance and timing of such instruction varies. Whereas some researchers are strongly against the teaching of individual letter-sound correspondences on the grounds that reading is about meaning, other authors argue that phonics teaching should begin on the first day in school.[23] So far, research studies have not addressed this question directly. However, a large number of research studies *have* addressed the question of when phonemic awareness emerges in the development of phonological skills. This research has suggested that knowledge about rimes emerges *prior* to knowledge about phonemes.

THE SEQUENCE OF PHONOLOGICAL DEVELOPMENT

One source of evidence about the relative difficulty of phonemic awareness in comparison to rime awareness comes from the studies of the development of rhyme discussed above. Research like Bradley and Bryant's[5,8] has shown that rhyme awareness develops early in young children, prior to their arrival in school, and is a strong predictor of how well they will eventually learn to read and to spell. In order to recognise that the non-rhyming word in a set of words like 'fan, cat, hat, mat' is *fan,* a child needs to be aware of two linguistic units, the rime, discussed previously, and the *onset.* Onsets correspond to the initial consonants in any English syllable. Onsets can either correspond to single phonemes, as in *c*at, *b*all and *f*ar, or to pairs (*st*ar, *tr*ip) or triples (*spr*ing, *str*ip) of phonemes.

Studies of the development of phonemic awareness, on the

other hand, have shown that an awareness of the constituent phonemes in words develops as children are learning to read. One of the earliest studies to show this was a study of phoneme deletion carried out by David Bruce.[24] Bruce asked children aged from 5 to 9 years of age to delete either the initial (*jam-am*), medial (*snail-sail*) or final (*fork-for*) phonemes from a set of 30 spoken words. He found that the 5- and 6-year-old children had great difficulty with this task. Performance only rose above chance levels when the children were aged 7 and 8, and had been learning to read for at least a year.

Another popular measure of phonemic awareness is the tapping task. In this task, which was devised by Isabelle Liberman and her colleagues, children are asked to tap once with a wooden dowel for each of the syllables or phonemes in spoken words.[25] The words in Liberman *et al.*'s task either had one syllable or phoneme (*dog, i*), two syllables or phonemes (*birthday, my*) or three syllables or phonemes (*valentine, red*). Liberman *et al.* found that young children could perform only the syllable task prior to learning to read. They were unable to tap out the number of phonemes in the different sets of words until they had been learning to read for about a year.

The results of both of these studies, and of many others[21], suggest that phonemic awareness is a *consequence* rather than a precursor of learning to read, If this is true, then the emergence of phonemic awareness would not depend on intellectual maturation *per se*, but on reading instruction. Furthermore, studies of Japanese children have suggested that it is instruction in an alphabetic language that is important for phonemic awareness to emerge.[26] Again, it is worth stressing that research on the developmental emergence of phonological skills is *neutral* about the point at which alphabetic instruction should be formally introduced. Such research simply shows that rimes are more accessible phonological units than phonemes for young children who are learning to read.

One prediction that follows from the idea that phonemic awareness is a consequence of learning to read is that difficulties in phonemic tasks should be demonstrated by adults who have never learned to read, as well as by young children. Adult illiterates are obviously cognitively mature, but if phonemic awareness is a consequence of reading, then they should find phoneme deletion tasks as difficult as young children do. This turns out to be the case. Jose Morais and his colleagues showed that in Portugal adults who had not learned to read as children performed very poorly in phonemic deletion tasks, whereas adults who could read did not.[27] This finding supports the view that the awareness of phonemes in children and adults arises as a consequence of learning to read. Phonemic awareness is *not* a precursor of reading.

The most critical test of the view that onset-rime awareness emerges prior to the awareness of phonemes, however, is to give phonological tasks at both the onset-rime and the phoneme level to the same set of subjects. If young children can perform a certain phonological task at the onset-rime level but not at the phonemic level, and if the same stimuli are used in both tasks, then this would show that phonemic awareness emerges later than onset-rime awareness in young children.

Such a study was carried out by Rebecca Treiman and Andrea Zukowski.[28] They used a 'same-different' judgement task, in which children were asked to say whether two words sounded the same or different at either the beginning or the end. The beginning task could either be performed on the basis of shared onsets (*plea, plank*) or shared initial phonemes (*plea, pray*). The end task could either be performed on the basis of shared rimes (*rat, cat*) or shared final phonemes (*rat, wit*). Treiman and Zukowski found that 4- and 5-year-old children were very successful in the onset-rime version of the same-different task, but had great difficulty with the phoneme version. It was only 6-year-olds, who had been learning to read for about a year, who showed equivalent levels of performance at the two phonological levels. This study shows very clearly that the awareness of onsets and rimes precedes the awareness of phonemes in the development of phonological skills.

IMPLICATIONS FOR THE TEACHING OF READING

The research reviewed so far in this chapter has demonstrated a series of interesting facts about the development of reading and the development of phonological skills. The first is that an awareness of rhyme, and of the linguistic units of onset and rime, develops prior to an awareness of phonemes. The second is that there is a strong and robust relationship between early rhyming skills and later reading development. The third is that early rhyming ability is partly linked to later reading via the use of rime analogies. A young child who can read the word 'light' can use an analogy to read a new word like 'fight', and children who have better rhyming skills are more likely to make this connection. Children who have poor rhyming skills tend to have reading difficulties, and do not show a spontaneous use of rime analogies.

One implication of this set of facts is that it would be beneficial to give *all* children lots of early experience with rhyme and alliteration before they begin learning to read, beginning in nursery school. This could either be achieved via the informal use of nursery rhymes and singing games, or could be supported by more formal methods such as teaching children to recognise the rhyming words in nursery rhymes, and playing alliteration games such as 'I Spy'. The goal of this early onset-rime experience would be to ensure that *every* child entered primary school with an adequate phonological foundation from which to tackle the task of learning to read.

A second implication is that, for many children, a useful way into reading is to emphasise the links between rhyming sounds and the spelling sequences in sets of words that reflect these rhyming sounds. These connections will usually be consistent in their spelling-sound correspondence, whereas teaching children to 'sound out' words letter-by-letter will demonstrate the many inconsistencies in written English. It is important to note that teaching spelling-to-sound correspondences via rhyme does teach the alphabetic principle. The advantage is that children can learn that the sounds within words that they find accessible on a cognitive level, namely onsets and rimes, are frequently represented by the *same* letters or groups of letters when the words are written down. Rhyme-based methods are already used informally by many teachers who teach their children to look out for 'word families'. Words like *ball, fall* and *wall* are in the same 'family' because they not only share a rhyming sound, but a spelling pattern. Words like *cat*, *cup* and *cold* are also in the same 'family', the family of words that share an onset. The consistent representation of certain sounds by certain letters or groups of letters within word families may provide a less confusing way of teaching beginning readers to understand how the alphabet works than teaching them to decode words letter-by-letter.

There is another reason, too, why a focus on rhyme can help to teach children the alphabetic principle. This is the large overlap between onset-rime skills and the development of phonemic knowledge. Many onsets in written English correspond to single phonemes, and so the development of onset-rime awareness will *in itself* help the development of phonemic awareness. In fact, the alphabet charts that are ubiquitous in most classrooms depend on exactly this principle. Children are taught the sounds of letters like b, c and d via the onsets of words like *b*all, *c*at and *d*uck. Thus the research on the importance of onset-rime skills does *not* imply that the sounds of the alphabet should not be taught to young children, as sometimes seems to be assumed.[23] In fact, the data on the early emergence of onset-rime awareness suggests that this is *exactly* how the alphabet *should* be taught; via the use of onsets. The idea that there is a sharp developmental division between the two types of knowledge is misleading, and a misrepresentation of current research findings.

A third implication of the facts outlined above is that young children should be explicitly taught how to use rime analogies in the classroom. Although some children, usually those with the best phonological skills, will make rime analogies without any prompting, many children will need help in using the spelling pattern of one word as a basis for reading another. Practice is all-important, and the best way to provide this is via rhyming stories. Books that make a comprehensive use of rhyme, such as Dr Seuss's 'Cat in the Hat' books, can be used as a vehicle for helping children to understand that when words rhyme, they frequently share a spelling pattern. Such stories can also be used to show children that the pronunciation of one word can often provide a clue to the pronunciation of another. If they know 'cat' then they can work out how to read 'hat'. These analogies can be explicitly modelled for children, using plastic letters to replace one onset with another (for example, swapping c and h to change 'cat' into 'hat', and so on).

In fact, training studies based on rime analogy instruction have shown that this may be a particularly useful method to use with children who are having difficulties in learning to read.[29,30] Some of this work has suggested that rime analogies are particularly effective with dyslexic children.[29] The reason seems to be that rime analogies teach these children the alphabetic principle at a cognitively more accessible level of phonology, the onset-rime level. Whereas children find it relatively simple to hear that 'string' rhymes with 'thing', they find it very difficult to hear the individual phonemes in these words. Thus a traditional phonics method, in which each word is sounded out letter-by-letter, makes the learning task particularly inaccessible to children with poor phonological skills. The 'sounding out' involved in phonemic instruction not only places a significant burden on a child's short-term memory, it also frequently fails to provide a good approximation of the sound of the target word. A word like 'string' or 'people' is not the sum of its letter-sound correspondences.

CONCLUSION

Early reading development in English children seems to be intimately connected with their knowledge of rhyme. Children who have good rhyming skills become better readers, and children who have reading difficulties tend to have a rhyming deficit. One possible explanation for the salience of rhyme is that the English orthography is more consistent in its representation of sound at the onset-rime level than at the level of the phoneme. So children who can focus on spelling units that correspond to rhymes will find the task of learning to read easier than children who cannot. One way of focusing on spelling units that correspond to rhymes is to categorise words on the basis of shared rimes, and to use rime analogies. Children with good rhyming skills use the most rime analogies, and so such analogies may be one important causal link between early rhyme awareness and later reading development.

––––––––––––––––––– *R*EFERENCES –––––––––––––––––––

1. Opie, I. and Opie, P. (1987) *The Lore and Language of Schoolchildren*, Oxford: Oxford University Press.
2. Chukovsky, K. (1963) *From Two to Five*, Berkeley: University of California Press.
3. Dowker, A. (1989) 'Rhymes and alliteration in poems elicited from young children' in *Journal of Child Language*, *16*, 181–202.
4. Lenel, J.C. and Cantor, J.H.(1981) 'Rhyme recognition and phonemic perception in young children' in *Journal of Psycholinguistic Research*, *10*, 57-68
5. Bradley, L. and Bryant, P.E. (1983) 'Categorising sounds and learning to read: A causal connection' in *Nature*, *310*, 419–421
6. Snowling, M.J., Hulme, C., Smith, A. and Thomas, J. (1994) 'The effects of phonemic similarity and list length on children's sound categorisation performance' in *Journal of Experimental Child Psychology*, *58*, 160–180
7. Lundberg, I., Olofsson, A. and Walls, S. (1980) 'Reading and spelling skills in the first school years predicted from phonemic awareness skills in kindergarten' in *Scandinavian Journal of Psychology*, *21*, 159–173
8. Bradley, L. and Bryant, P.E. (1978) 'Difficulties in auditory organisation as a possible cause of reading backwardness' in *Nature*, *271*, 746–747
9. Stanback, M.L. (1992) 'Syllable and rime patterns for teaching reading: Analysis of a frequency-based vocabulary of 17,602 words' in *Annals of Dyslexia*, *42*, 196–221
10. Wylie, R.E. and Durrell, D.D. (1970) *Elementary English*, *47*, 787–791.
11. Treiman, R. (1988) 'The internal structure of the syllable' in G. Carlson and M. Tanenhaus (eds.), *Linguistic structure in language processing* (pp.27–52). Dordrecht, The Netherlands: Kluger.
12. Goswami, U. (1986) 'Children's use of analogy in learning to read: A development study' in *Journal of Experimental Child Psychology*, *42*, 73–83
13. Goswami, U. (1988) 'Orthographic analogies and reading development' in *Quarterly Journal of Experimental Psychology*, *40A*, 239–268

14. Goswami, U. (1990) 'A special link between rhyming skills and the use of orthographic analogies by beginning readers' in *Journal of Child Psychology and Psychiatry, 31*, 301–311
15. Goswami, U. (1991) 'Learning about spelling sequences: The role of onsets and rimes in analogies in reading' in *Child Development, 62*, 1110–1123
16. Goswami, U, (1993) 'Towards an interactive Analogy Model of Reading Development: Decoding vowel graphemes in beginning reading' in *Journal of Experimental Child Psychology, 56*, 443–475
17. Morais, J., Cary, L., Alegria, J and Bertelson, P. (1979) 'Does awareness of speech as a sequence of phonemes arise spontaneously?' in *Cognition, 7*, 323–331
18. Goswami, U. and Mead, F. (1992) 'Onset and rime awareness and analogies in reading' in *Reading Research Quarterly, 27* (2), 152–162
19. Lovett, M.W., Warren-Chaplin, P.M., Ransby, M.J. and Borden, S.L. (1990) 'Training the word recognition skills of dyslexic children: Treatment and transfer effects' in *Journal of Educational Psychology, 82*, 769–780
20. Muter, V., Snowling, M.J. and Taylor, S. (1994) 'Orthographic analogies and phonological awareness: Their role and significance in early reading development' in *Journal of Child Psychology and Psychiatry, 35*, 293–310
21. Goswami, U. and Bryant, P.E. (1990) *Phonological Skills and Learning to Read.* Hillsdale, NJ: Lawrence Erlbaum
22. Cataldo, S. and Ellis, N.C. (1988) 'Interactions in the development of spelling, reading and phonological skills' in *Journal of Research in Reading, 11*(2), 86–109
23. Chew, J. (1994) *Professional Expertise and Parental Experience in the Teaching of Reading, or Mother Often Knows Best.* York: Campaign for Real Education
24. Bruce, D.J. (1964) 'The analysis of word sounds' in *British Journal of Educational Psychology, 34*, 158–70
25. Liberman, I.Y., Shankweiler, D., Fischer, F.W. and Carter, B. (1974) 'Explicit syllable and phoneme segmentation in the young child' in *Journal of Experimental Child Psychology, 18*, 201–212
26. Mann, V.A. (1986) 'Phonological awareness: The role of reading experience' in *Cognition, 24*, 65–92

27. Content, A., Morais, J., Alegria, J. and Bertelson, P. (1982) 'Accelerating the development of phonetic segmentation skills in kindergarteners' in *Cahiers de Psychologie Cognitive, 2,* 259–269

28. Gaskins, I.W., Downer, M.A. and Gaskins, R.W. (1986) *Introduction to the Benchmark School word identification/ vocabulary development program.* Media, PA: Benchmark Press

29. Treiman, R. and Zukowski, A. (1991) 'Levels of Phonological Awareness' in S. Brady and D. Shankweiler (eds.) *Phonological Processes in Literacy.* Hillsdale, NJ: Erlbaum

30. White, T.G. and Cunningham, P.M. (1990) *Teaching disadvantaged students to decode by analogy.* Paper presented at the annual meeting of the American Educational Research Association, Boston, MA, April 1990.

RHYME IN CHILDREN'S WRITING

Sandy Brownjohn

> *There was a young man of Japan,*
> *Who wrote verses that never would scan,*
> *When folk told him so,*
> *He replied: 'Yes, I know,*
> *But I always try and get as many words*
>   *into the last line as I possibly can'*
>
> Anon

THE 'MOON, JUNE, PRUNE' SYNDROME

> *I walked beneath the silvery moon*
> *In the merry month of June,*
> *And then ... I ate a stewed prune!*

Rhyme is a problem for children when they begin writing their own poems, and it is not really surprising. They are often battling with their own, and their teachers', preconceived ideas of what constitutes a poem.

Nursery rhymes have been their earliest introduction to the power of rhyme, and it *is* a magical power, and it seems natural to assume that rhyme is what makes the real difference between poetry and prose. Many teachers, too, know little about the range of techniques which can be employed by poets. It is not their fault. Poetry as a craft has rarely been taught in schools or colleges, and rhyme is the easiest and most obvious of these techniques to identify. Thus, the idea that all poems have to rhyme or they are not poems, has wide currency. By 'rhyme' here, we are talking about full rhyme at the ends of lines only, as in

> *Little Polly Flinders*
> *Sat among the cinders ...*

However, this is only one way of using rhyme in a poem; but more of that later.

The lure of such rhyme is very understandable. After all, poetry used to be an oral art, a spoken music, and rhyme chimes on the ear to charm and delight the listener. It sings in the memory and its harmonies help us to recall what we have heard. Notice how many nursery characters have rhyming names: Humpty Dumpty, Incey Wincey Spider, Henny Penny; popular comic characters, too, like Beryl the Peril and Dennis the Menace. Abracadabra and Hocus Pocus also acknowledge this magical power of rhyme. Even as adults we still enjoy coining rhyming compounds like pooper-scooper, arty-farty, wheeler-dealer and gender-bender.

Those writing poetry for children almost always use end-stop rhyme; sometimes, it has to be said, producing little more than jingles which entertain briefly but do not enhance or further children's knowledge of what language can achieve, or encourage them to deeper thought.

It is a little wonder that children's early efforts at writing poetry are often banal and superficial. What they may have to say becomes distorted and disappears under the dictates of the first rhyming word that comes to mind, resulting in the 'moon, June, prune' syndrome.

But poetry, according to Coleridge, is 'the best words in the best order'[1], and as such it offers one of the most effective means for people to express their deepest thoughts and ideas in writing. Children's writing should be original and individual. We want to encourage them to be adventurous and innovative in their poetry, not safe and derivative, and in order to be able to do this they deserve to be taught the craft and language techniques to help them to shape their ideas effectively. So it is to the teachers, first of all, that we must turn to make sure that *they* are aware of these various techniques so that they can pass them on in their classrooms.

Unfortunately, there is a disturbing trend away from the study of poetry in schools, colleges and universities, and what little remains is usually dealt with on a purely literary level with scant reference to the actual craft of writing, and even less opportunity actually to write oneself. Learning by doing is still the most efficient way of mastering a subject, of understanding its full potential, and of being able to appreciate what is produced by others in the same field. ·

WHAT IS RHYME?

True education is the 'drawing out' of what is already there, whether it be knowledge, the ability to reason, or natural talent. The main task, therefore, would seem to be to make sure that the educators, the 'drawers out', know what they are hoping to find. So, what *are* we looking for with regard to rhyme?

Young children have already experienced, through nursery rhymes and songs, most of the different rhyming techniques they will need to know. Unfortunately, although their teachers know them too, usually neither group knows that it knows. In order to be able to use these techniques consciously in later writing, children need to have some *explicit* knowledge (which is not to say that they cannot employ them intuitively or instinctively). So, if their teachers are aware of the possibilities, they will be in a better position to guide and enlighten their pupils. Since nursery rhymes and songs are the main sources of our implicit knowledge, it makes sense to extract from these early experiences the range of ways open to a writer to use rhyme.

Most of the craft of writing poetry could be said to divide into three broad areas – rhyme, rhythm and image. I define rhyme in this broad context as employing linguistic effects which chime on the ear, and these may run the gamut from full rhyme right through to alliteration. This chiming of sound on the ear can be achieved by various means, many of which have their counterparts in music, the most obvious being repetition.

Repetition

Repetition is an exact echo of sound; the same word, phrase or line returns in the poem unchanged, so our ears pick up the rhyme. The following example uses repetition as the basis for

its rhyme (along with rhythm, which is not, however, my brief
in this chapter).

> *Polly put the kettle on,*
> *Polly put the kettle on,*
> *Polly put the kettle on,*
> *We'll all have tea.*
> *Sukey take it off again,*
> *Sukey take it off again,*
> *Sukey take it off again,*
> *They've all gone away.*

We can see this device at work in music as a chorus or refrain,
or as a theme that runs through a composition (e.g. rondo),
or as a pattern of notes that recurs. These are particularly
noticeable in the construction of nursery rhymes and folk
songs. Sing 'Humpty Dumpty' to yourself and listen to the first
and third lines of music, or 'Ten Green Bottles' where it is the
first and fourth lines which repeat the same tune.

Poems share many effects with music, for instance rhyme and
harmony are linked, as are metrical feet and time signatures.
We are familiar with the idea of a chorus or refrain as is
evident in the following example where almost all the rhyme
in the whole piece is achieved through repetition.

> *Old MacDonald had a farm, E-I-E-I-O*
> *And on that farm he had a cow, E-I-E-I-O*
> *With a moo moo here, And a moo moo there*
> *Here a moo, there a moo, everywhere a moo moo*
> *Old MacDonald had a farm, E-I-E-I-O*

The refrain can be seen at work in many forms of poems,
including the villanelle, roundel, rondeau and ballade[2], most
of which have their origins in music and song.

Part repetition

Part repetition also allows a rhyming echo, although some of
the words (or tune) have been changed. If we consider 'Ten
Green Bottles' again, we obviously notice the number change
in the fourth line of each verse. However, more interesting
musically is the transposition of the note pattern from line one
into line two, where it is repeated, but in a slightly higher
register. In poetry that option is not open to us, but we can do

a similar thing using the same pattern of language and making subtle changes. For example,

> Incey Wincey spider climbed up the spout,
> Down came the rain and *washed the spider out;*
> Out came the sun and *dried up all the rain,*
> Incey Wincey spider climbed the spout again.

Single word repetition

Single word repetition can also play an important role in helping to make a poem effective. For example,

> *There was a* crooked *man*
> *Who walked a* crooked *mile,*
> *He found a* crooked *sixpence*
> *Against a* crooked *stile ...*

Probably the best-known example in modern poetry of the use of this device is Charles Causley's 'I Saw A Jolly Hunter'[3], where the word 'jolly' occurs in seventeen of the twenty lines of the poem, with subtle changes in shades of meaning each time.

NB The main thing to remember with repetition is that it should always be intended and should add to the meaning of the poem. It should never be used through a mistaken belief that it will make a piece of writing sound 'more poetic' (whatever that is). Thus, it is not generally advisable to repeat the first line of a poem as the last line, in an attempt to round it all off, unless there is a very good reason for doing so.

Full rhyme

Full rhyme is what most people mean when they talk about rhyme. It is when two or more words sound exactly the same in essence, only the beginnings are different, as in 'the c*at* s*at* on the m*at*'.

Full end-stop rhyme

Full end-stop rhyme (what Tom McArthur calls 'end rhyme' in Chapter 2) is when these full rhyming words occur at the ends of lines and complete a unit of thought. As has already been stated, most early experiences of nursery rhymes and songs appear to reinforce the notion that full end-stop rhyme is the *only* kind of rhyme that counts. For example,

Pussy cat, pussy cat, where have you been?
I've been up to London to look at the queen.
Pussy cat, pussy cat, what did you there?
I frightened a little mouse under the chair.

Unfortunately, trying to rhyme in this way can be very restricting for children attempting to grapple with all the demands of producing a poem that actually says something which has meaning for both them and their readers. Some English words, it is true, have many one-word full rhymes, but others have very few, and some have none at all, for example, silver, secret, sausage.

Rhyming one word with two

Rhyming one word with two is a slightly more sophisticated way of finding a rhyme. It occurs, though not exclusively, in light verse. For example,

Little Miss Muffet
Sat on a tuffet,
Eating her curds and whey,
There came a big spider
Who sat down beside her,
And frightened Miss Muffet away.

Internal full rhyme

Internal full rhyme offers more scope for a writer. Internal rhyme is where the rhyming words occur anywhere within, say, one or two lines of a poem, within the body of the poem, so that the ear hears them. *Not* having to end lines with rhymes gives a writer much more flexibility. The internal rhyme is an added texture and will be picked up by the ear, but will enable the writer to have more choice of when and where to use rhyme. For example,

Mary, Mary, *quite* contrary,
How does your garden grow?
With silver bells and cockle shells
And pretty maids all in a row.

The following five sections are examples of what Tom McArthur calls 'Rhyme-1' in Chapter 2.

Half (part, or near) rhyme

Half (part, or near) rhyme is fairly self-explanatory. Half rhymes are words that partly chime on the ear but do not rhyme fully, for example, single, angle and jungle. They might be examples of assonance where words contain a repeated vowel sound. For example,

> Peter, Peter, *Pumpkin* eater,
> *Had a wife and couldn't* keep her, ...

or

> *Oranges and* lemons,
> *Say the bells of St.* Clements,
> *You owe me five* farthings,
> *Say the bells of St.* Martins, ...

Or they might be examples of *consonance* where it is consonants that repeat the sound, for example, trick, truck, track and trek.

> *Doctor Foster went to Gloucester*
> *In a shower of rain;*
> *He stepped in a* puddle,
> *Right up to his* middle,
> *And never went there again.*

As with full rhymes, half rhymes can be placed either at the ends of lines or be used internally. Half rhymes offer children much greater scope in their writing as there are obviously many more examples of half rhymes in English, and also there are always children who find it difficult when they first begin writing to hear full rhymes.

Assonance

Assonance is the repeated vowel sounds within words near each other in the poem, which may or may not occur at the ends of lines. For example,

> *Little Bo-Peep, has lost her sheep,*
> *And doesn't know where to find them.*
> *Leave them alone and they'll come home,*
> *Bringing their tails behind them.*

or

> *Pat-a-cake, pat-a-cake, baker's man* ...

Consonance

Consonance is the repeated consonant sound within words near each other in the poem, which may or may not occur at the ends of lines. For example,

> ... P*at* it and p*r*ick it and ma*r*k it with B ...

or

> *Hickory, dickory, dock,*
> *The mouse ran up the clock,*
> *The clock struck one ...*

Alliteration

Alliteration is well known as a poetic device, if only through the tongue twisters that children hear when young. For example,

> P*eter* P*ip*er p*icked a p*eck of p*ickled p*epper ...

It is less often realised that it belongs in the area of rhyme. Alliteration is best seen as the repetition of initial sounds occurring before stressed syllables; in practice this usually means the first letter(s) of a word, but not always. As the sound is repeated in words near each other in the poem, albeit only a letter or two, we hear it as a tiny rhyme which adds to the musical texture of the piece. For example,

> *Little* B*oy* B*lue come* b*low up your horn,*
> *The sheep's in the meadow, the* c*ow's in the* c*orn ...*

or

> B*aa* b*aa* b*lack sheep*

and

> S*ing a* s*ong of* s*ixpence*

Spelling (or eye) rhyme

Spelling (or eye) rhyme (what Tom McArthur calls 'imperfect rhyme' in Chapter 2) does not occur very often but it is worth knowing that it exists. Such rhymes look on the page as if they will sound the same because of their spelling, but when pronounced they sound different. Therefore, this kind of rhyme could almost be said to be academic, although it often gives rise to half rhymes as in the example below.

There were two crows sat on a stone,
One flew away and then there was one,
The other seeing his neighbour gone,
He flew away and then there were none.

All the above are the principal kinds of rhyme which children already 'know' and which they can use in their writing. The list is not absolutely complete, and has been simplified in some instances, but contains enough possibilities for any teacher to explore with pupils.

In the classroom

When children begin to write using rhyme, we generally find that either the scansion (or rhythm) works but the meaning is lost, or the rhyme works in conjunction with the meaning and the scansion goes out of the window. Both these broad areas of rhyme and rhythm are very demanding individually. Attempting to do both at the same time (and still write something worth saying) without any guidance or practice in each separately, can be asking children to do too much too soon.

My experience has shown that when children start to write poetry it is probably best, in these early stages, to discourage the use of rhyme altogether. It is essential at first for children to realise that *what* they have to say is rather more important than how they say it. Of course, this is only the beginning. Eventually, they must learn to marry the two and explore the techniques of the craft to help their meaning come through more effectively.

Since many children automatically go into rhyme mode at the mere mention of the word 'poetry', it is often helpful to introduce them to poetic forms which do not employ rhyme, like the syllabic forms of Haiku, Tanka and Cinquains.[4] The fact that these forms exist, and even have exotic-sounding names, can lend legitimacy to non-rhyming poetry in children's eyes.

Whichever way teachers approach poetry writing with their classes, the main aim at the outset should be to build up children's confidence in using language. They must learn to be adventurous and to take charge of the words they use. Too often their writing reflects the exact opposite of this. For example, they tend to use only the words they know how to spell; or they write superficially, employing trite or hackneyed phrases. Trying to use rhyme, as has already been stated, can result in pieces where the first rhyme that occurs dictates the content; or the rhythm and word order can become tortuous to accommodate the rhyme.

The best way I have found to help to build this confidence is to play word games of different kinds and to try writing about specific ideas which encourage the use of the imagination within a supportive framework or pattern. I have set many of these down at greater length in my books, *To Rhyme Or Not To Rhyme?* and *Word Games*[5]; the following are just two of the possible ideas that teachers might try when (re)introducing children to the use of rhyme.

Playing with full rhyme

One of the best games for allowing children to practise the use of full rhyme can be played orally at first and followed up in writing. 'I'd rather ... than ...' is played as a group, each member taking it in turns to supply a line that rhymes with the first statement. For example,

> *(1st player) I'd rather be silver than* gold.
> *(2nd player) I'd rather be young than* old.
> *(3rd player) I'd rather run away than be* bold ...

This continues until no one can think of another line, the last person to speak being the winner.

The thought processes involved are as follows. Firstly, we run through the alphabet in our minds putting different consonants in front of the rhyme '-old'. Then we try blends of consonants, like '*sc*old'. Thirdly, we try to find two (or more) syllable words, like 'behold' or 'marigold'. Having found a possible rhyme, we then have to construct a statement (I'd rather ... than ...) in which the first element bears some relation to the second, to the rhyming word. This is not always so easy.

As this shows, wider aspects of language are being addressed at the same time as giving children the opportunity to learn which sounds in English have many rhymes, which have few, and which have none at all. The statement, 'I'd rather be gold than silver', for example, would be an outright winner in this game because, to the best of my knowledge, there are no one-word rhymes for 'silver'.

> *I'd rather be an honest man than a knave,*
> *I'd rather have a six-foot beard than shave,*
> *I'd rather spend it all than try to save,*
> *I'd rather live in a house than in a cave,*
> *I'd rather be cremated than buried in a grave,*
> *I'd rather play with teddy than be brave.*
> Extract from a written version by a Y6 girl

Introducing alliteration

Taking the numbers one to ten and writing an alliterative, often surreal, sentence for each number, can be an enjoyable exercise that enables children to practise the technique whilst having fun at the same time; and we should never forget the fun we can have with language.

> *One waggly walrus won a wet wager,*
> *Two trustful twins tumbled into a typhoon,*
> *Three thin thoroughbreds thumped a thick thief,*
> *Four fiddly ferns ferociously ate a ferret,*
> *Five fervent fleas sat famished in a farm,*
> *Six shy shuttlecocks swam in shampoo,*
> *Seven stupid strawberries sinned on a stripey stretcher,*
> *Eight echoing earthquakes exterminated an eclipse,*
> *Nine nosy nomads knitted knotted knickers,*
> *Ten topless toffees told a tale.*
> Y5 children

A 'game' like this can also encourage children to use dictionaries. They only have to find the relevant letter-sound section in order to have access to a treasure chest of words to use in these sentences, as the children in the above example did with great pleasure.

By overdoing the alliteration at this point, children become very familiar with the technique. Later, they will use it more sparingly to add texture to their writing. For example,

... The breeze covered every corner
And heaved at every hedge.
It flustered every field
And shook the shed made of wood ...
                Extract from 'The Breeze', Y6 girl

ASSONANCE AND CONSONANCE

More often than not examples of these devices will occur
naturally in children's writing without their having prior
explicit knowledge of them. As long as teachers are aware of
these techniques, they will be able to point out to children
when they have used them. At first it is almost always better to
use children's own work as a teaching aid wherever possible. It
will delight them to know that they have used a particular
technique and this will be the moment when they are most
receptive to being told how it works and being given the
correct terminology. This is why it is so important that teachers
know what to look for. Apart from the alliteration in the
following pattern poem, there are example of full rhyme and
assonance.

I'm sat at the top of the tallest tree,
Watching the badgers bustling busily,
Watching the magpies eagerly steal,
Watching the squirrels scrambling dangerously,
Watching the family over their meal,
Watching the hunter load his gun,
Watching the rabbits in the midday sun.
                Y6 boy

The next extract from a poem entitled 'Ode To A Jelly Tot'
also includes examples of a repeated language pattern,
alliteration, full rhyme and consonance (arguably
onomatopoeic here, i.e. reproducing the sound of eating).

... Never shall I touch another toffee,
Never shall I chew another fudge,
Never shall I chomp another chocolate,
Never shall I gulp another gobstopper,
Never shall I absorb another aniseed ball,
Never shall I gobble another piece of gum,

Never shall I crunch another candy stick,
Never shall I munch another Mars bar.
Never shall I swallow another inferior sweet -
Without you my life wouldn't be complete.

Y6 girl

REPETITION, HALF RHYME AND INTERNAL RHYME

GRANDAD

A quiet man,
A thinking man,
Always down in his shed
Working on a broken clock
Or fixing a car instead.
A quiet man,
A thinking man,
But now he's dead.

Y6 girl

This seemingly simple poem, about a real event, is full of examples of the conscious use of different techniques and took this ten-year-old girl some time to complete. The use of repetition here plays an important part in helping to build a picture of the man. At first it introduces us to him as a simple statement of fact (A quiet man,/A thinking man,). When the lines are repeated they play a slightly different role. Not only do they help to give a structure to the poem, but the tone is now more reflective and serves to emphasise the feeling of loss as they lead to the final rhyme. Rhyming ('shed', 'instead' and 'dead') does not occur in every line and the earlier couplet signals the final, strongest rhyme of the three, 'dead'. As this is the last word it has the effect of turning us back to the rest of the poem, making sense of it, as it were, in retrospect.

The selection of details to describe her grandad is also significant. It is often what a poet chooses to leave out that can be almost as important as what s/he includes. Writing poems about strong emotions like loss can be difficult to do, and many children (and adults) fall into the trap of telling us how upset they are, of letting it all 'hang out'. But if we do this we erect a barrier between us and our readers; all we let them do, at best, is sympathise and look on us with pity. We have done all the crying for them. It is far better to tell the facts, using carefully selected details, so that through these, and the way we express them, we can involve readers to engage with the poem and experience our feelings too.

The following extract from a poem entitled 'Caterpillar' contains examples of half rhyme, internal rhyme, assonance and alliteration, all consciously deployed within the same poem by a Y6 boy.

> *Crawls like a miniature* ocean,
> *Arriving at an unknown destin*ation,
> *Tenderly feels around a* leaf,
> *Every contact is* brief, *as if entering a naked flame.*
> *... Ignorant of the prodding* hand
> *Leans, and falls to* land *upon a leaf below ...*

Using different examples of rhyme (whether full, internal, half or any other) only occasionally in poems, rather than attempting to rhyme throughout, can encourage children to experiment without losing sight of what they are trying to say. This gives a freedom and scope which will not undermine their growing confidence, and will remove the sometimes insuperable problems of sustaining rhyme all the way through which can lead children to lose heart and give up.

As they become more proficient in handling rhyme and other poetic techniques they can be introduced to some of the established rhyming forms, like Rondelets, Ottava Rima, Clerihews and Sonnets.[4] There is no doubt that these are within the capabilities of older primary children, *if* they have received enlightened and informed teaching throughout their career, probably arising from a committed school policy on the teaching of poetry. The more opportunity to practise techniques within a context that allows for mistakes – indeed, which recognises that the greatest learning often comes from a failure to succeed – the more children will become confident users of their medium. Their new explicit knowledge will fuse with the implicit and instinctive, providing them with a bank of experience on which they can draw at will, and often intuitively, in order to give the most effective voice to their creative talent.

It is worth ending with an example of a sonnet (employing both half and full rhymes) which was written by a Y6 boy who took a month to redraft it, on and off, both at school and at home. It became so important to him to complete that he was not willing to let it go until he had brought it as near perfection as he was able. There are lapses in the strict rhythm of the sonnet but it runs well when spoken and the spirit is there. It is a fairly chilling piece and leaves us wondering quite who or what the 'joker' is a metaphor for; conscience, experience, death?

THE FOUR MEN

The man approached the place of the four men.
You come to take my sleep? said the sleeper;
I do not want your sleep, so sleep again.
You come to take my food? said the eater;
I do not want your food, I have enough.
Do you come for my thoughts? said the thinker;
I do not want your thoughts, your thoughts may bluff.
Do you come for my drink? said the drinker;
I have no thirst so drink all that you can.
I am the joker and I come to fool,
I shall keep joking as when life began.
I'll take your heart and stuff it till it's full,
I'll take your brains and carve them with my knife,
And what I come for, I shall steal – your life.

Such a commitment to writing is surely what all teachers want to encourage. Working in this way, at this level, children learn more about language than any grammar exercise can ever hope to offer. They learn to be in charge of their thoughts and words, to flex their language muscles and to realise the power and confidence this can bring. When they have something to say, and it matters to them to say it as well as they can, they will 'worry' at their poems until they have found the 'best words in the best order,' and, in the process, will experience the deep satisfaction and magical excitement which accompany the successful completion of any creative endeavour.

*R*EFERENCES

1. 'I wish our clever young poets would remember my homely definitions of prose and poetry; that is, prose = words in their best order; poetry = the best words in the best order.' Samuel Taylor Coleridge, *Table Talk*, 12 July 1827
2. For more information on poetic forms see Stillman, F. (1966) *The Poet's Manual and Rhyming Dictionary*. London: Thames and Hudson
3. 'I Saw a Jolly Hunter', from Causley, C. (1970) *Figgie Hobbin*, London: Macmillan
4. Forms described in Brownjohn, S. (1994) *To Rhyme Or Not To Rhyme?* London: Hodder and Stoughton
5. Brownjohn, S. and Whitaker, J. (1994) *Word Games* (second edition). London: Hodder and Stoughton.

6

🟦🟦🟦🟦🟦🟦🟦🟦🟦🟦🟦🟦🟦🟦🟦🟦🟦🟦🟦🟦🟦🟦🟦🟦🟦🟦🟦🟦🟦🟦🟦🟦🟦🟦

RHYMING POETRY FOR CHILDREN

Brian Morse

> *Words?*
> *Why he could almost make 'em talk.*
>   Roger McGough, *Poem For A Dead Poet*

'Poems? They rhyme' is the invariable response when you ask a junior class the first thing that comes into their heads when you mention the word *poetry*. But usually there are second thoughts, 'But they don't have to, do they?'

Poetry has its fashions, as does everything else, and once, in the good old days, children's poetry – almost at deliberate odds with what was happening in the 'realer' world of adult poetry – rhymed. And that was that. Then, in the late seventies, a modernising wind blew in. It became more acceptable, indeed rather fashionable, not to rhyme (Michael Rosen's and Ted Hughes's poems, though written from very different standpoints, remain the prime examples). Since then the pendulum has swung back (as it has in the world of adult British poetry). Most poetry written for children in recent years rhymes, and quite adventurously at times because during the eighties there was a further trend, that of adult practitioners (though this is no automatic guarantee of success) trying their hand at writing for a younger audience. The daring idea that poetry need not rhyme and can be organised by other devices has, by and large, not caught on.

This survey of poetry deals therefore with poetry that is, in the main, rhyming. It begins with later Victorian poets and finishes with some very recent poets. Children's poetry, however, is not a homogenous subject; younger children have their poets, as do older children, though the audience for the bulk of writers is, roughly, the eight- to twelve-year-olds. And in the last few years Grace Nichols[1,2], John Agard[1,3] and, for older children, James Berry[4] have added a further dimension, the strong influence of Caribbean verse. One thing, however, has not changed so very much over the last hundred years; with a few notable exceptions the best poetry for children is produced by writers who primarily write for adults.

Reading books of poems

Every book we open is a risk we take. We may be so overwhelmed by what we read that our lives are changed. On the other hand we may throw the text aside in utter boredom or incomprehension. It is a sobering thought that in theory one particular text may be the reason for our becoming a non-reader.

Books, however, take even larger risks with readers. This is especially so with books of verse and child readers who have perhaps been attracted by the cover or been made a recommendation by an adult. For a book of poems is different from a book of prose and children need to be told so. Most children are taught to read by means of short, then longer prose narratives. But prose, short story, novel or a technical work, is intended to be read from first page to last, with perhaps a glance back to clarify some point, or a glance ahead to see what happens next, while a book of poems is meant to be dipped into, put down, picked up again. A poem that seems too difficult or initially uninviting can be left for later, maybe for ever. You may re-read a poem several times, then flick several poems ahead or behind. A book of poetry is a collection of perhaps thirty or forty separate acts of inspiration: readers need to learn to accept that they will enjoy some more than others, that some are more difficult, some yield their meaning if not their enjoyment only after several readings. As adults we put a poetry collection aside and come back to it over a period of days and weeks and years: it is a funfair and not a static exhibition to be moved through from entrance to exit or a series of hurdles, all of which have to be overcome in order.

To give readers and the book of poems a chance, therefore, the poems and the children who grow towards reading them (and then grow out of them: I have the rest of my life to come to terms with *The Cantos* or *The Ring And The Book*, but children have perhaps only three or four years in which they and a particular book are suited) need constant reminding of the special nature of a book of poems. Children also need to be told something of what to expect from the particular book, perhaps steered towards key poems. In most books the tone of the individual poems, even though they are by the same author, will not be consistent. A collection is likely to contain sad and serious poems mixed in with comic verses. One poem can be simultaneously both wildly amusing and deadly serious and it is far more likely than a piece of prose to contain a sudden difficult word or an unfamiliar reference: how many of us as adults have not been 'stuck' on a line, a verse, a single phrase of a poem? And the voices in the poems; each poem will have its own. Which is not even to mention the forms poems may take.

And when was the poem written? It may not be immediately obvious that the book was written long ago. Some of Robert Louis Stevenson's poems might have been almost written yesterday, or a least at no particular time ...

> '*Whenever the moon and stars are set,*
> *Whenever the wind is high,.*
> *All night long in the dark and wet,*
> *A man goes riding by —*'[5]

... but others with their nursery references and lamplights and assumption about emperors and kings can, despite what has been learnt from the National Curriculum, seem plain out-of-date. There are fashions in how much cultural and historical contexts are relevant to the appreciation of literature, but a little explanation of Stevenson's personal circumstances and the way middle-class Victorian children were brought up may help breathe life into the poems that they deserve. Likewise many of Gareth Owen's poems, only published in the 1980s – Stevenson's *A Child's Garden Of Verses* appeared in 1885 – often refer to a terraced street way of life and community that is fast disappearing, if it hasn't already disappeared.

We always stand behind the goal
In the middle of the roar.
The others come to see the game—
I come for Denis Law.

The poem 'Denis Law' the with its references to Jimmy
Greaves and Bobby Charlton may be totally obvious to anyone
over thirty, even if they have no interest in sport, but not
necessarily to an eight-year-old. Just a few words from an adult
may help to connect the almost gone to now.

Children also need to hear how poems sound, whether out
loud or in the privacy of their heads. It is common to hear a
child who obviously relishes poetry reading a poem aloud,
perhaps from a scheme reading book, as if it was prose,
reading it with an utter disregard for the form of the poem, as
if poetry whether free verse or rhymed was not written in lines,
as if the rhymes were there by accident, as if there was no
music involved. Rhyme, rhythm, verses, lines, images – these
are all technical terms, and we might substitute other words
for children, but many children can cope with them (they do
in poetry workshops when writing for themselves) and if they
are aware of them we will be adding to their enjoyment of the
poetry they read.

TRADITIONAL FIGURES AND COMIC WRITERS

Once there was a trilogy, *A Child's Garden Of Verses*, *A Puffin
Quartet of Poets* and *The Book Of A Thousand Poems*, and every
school in the land had at least one copy of each book, the
latter in the Teachers' Reference section in the staffroom. No
Please, Mrs Butler[7], no *Quick, Let's Get Out Of Here*[8], no *Season
Songs*[9]. The real quarrel, however, with the school-bound view
of poetry for children that persisted well into the seventies
must be that in the case of Stevenson, *A Child's Garden* contains
some marvellously crafted and haunting poems – who would
be without 'Windy Nights', 'From A Railway Carriage' or 'The
Swing'? – but it is a repetitious volume with many lesser pieces,
and there is more to Stevenson's poetry than this volume, for
example 'Christmas at Sea'.

> *The sheets were frozen hard, and they cut the naked hand;*
> *The decks were like a slide, where a seaman scarce could stand ...*

In the case of Victorian poetry in general no publisher looked beyond the view of it imposed by the Opies' *Oxford Book Of Children's Verse*[10] : there is a considerable body of work by, for example, the American James Whitcomb Riley (despite 'Little Orphan Annie' something of a Rosen of his day) or the Irishman William Allingham, writer not only of 'The Fairies' but also of poems such as

> *The boy from his bedroom-window*
> *Look'd over the little town,*
> *And away to the bleak black upland*
> *Under a clouded moon*

which got mislaid from the canon of poetry for children. In the case of Eleanor Graham's *Quartet*[11] which contains poems by Eleanor Farjeon, James Reeves, E.V. Rieu and Ian Serraillier, except for Reeves (better seen in his *Complete Poems For Children*)[12] , the poets are small beer, pedestrian versifiers of less than consummate craftsmanship.

Other poets worth looking at from this earlier period of poetry for children (and perhaps controversially I am taking 1970, the year of publication of Charles Causley's *Figgie Hobbin*[13] , as the watershed after which the present children's poetry 'scene' started) would include, of course, Christina Rossetti for *Sing-Song*[14] , nursery rhyme type poems, and *Goblin Market*[15] , a simple and sinister narrative, recommended for older readers, and Walter de la Mare, ill-served by the standard offering, *Peacock Pie*, but a far more exciting poet when you dip into his unfortunately sparsely illustrated *Collected Rhymes and Verses.*[16]

Many of the standard comic texts by Belloc, Lear, Carroll and Nash also belong to the pre-1970 period. Belloc, from the turn of the century, can be read in *Selected Cautionary Tales*[17] , the American Nash in *Custard and Company*[18] , Lear in *A Book of Nonsense*[19] , but his fellow Victorian Carroll will have to be found in the *Alice* books or anthologised. Mervyn Peake's *Rhymes Without Reason*[20] (illustrated by the author and published in 1944) is both a superb integration of word and image and perhaps the funniest, saddest, most comical, most tragical book you could dip into. It is short and his verses are hypnotically memorable. His characters range from 'My Uncle Paul of Pimlico' who has

> ... *seven cats as white as snow,*
> *Who sit at his enormous feet*
> *And watch him, as a special treat*

to the walrus along whose

> ... *weary whiskers*
> *The tears flow fast and free.*
> *They twinkle in the Arctic*
> *And plop into the sea.*

T.S. Eliot's *Old Possum's Book Of Practical Cats*[21] comes from 1939. Whether you enjoy the poems or find them altogether arch and adult is a question of personal taste. *Meet My Folks!*[22] is Ted Hughes's contribution to the humorous (and in this case rhyming) market. To my mind a good few of the poems rather lumber but as a volume it has run and run. A.A. Milne's *When We Were Very Young*[23], the better of his volumes, has, of course, run even further; there have been well over a hundred reprints since 1924. Milne constructs his poems marvellously, has a tremendous ear for metre and for the sounds words make, and he is above all clear: no wasted words or padding. He is also, and to my mind unfairly, associated with a somewhat cosy mothers-knee view of poetry. Like many other poets from an age gone by, he deserves a more modern illustrator than Ernest Shepard who, one suspects, was not exactly the most contemporary of interpreters in his own day.

Other comic verse writers, some of them quite recent, you might wish to look at would include Max Fatchen, Colin West, Adrian Henri, Richard Edwards, Spike Milligan and the Americans Shel Silverstein and Jack Prelutsky.

POETRY BOOKS FOR YOUNGER CHILDREN

Traditionally children of the four- to eight-year-old age group (of course the lower and upper ages are flexible – reading and/or interest ages for poems are obviously difficult to judge: you may alter your judgement the very next time a child opens a book or you read to one) have been served by Mother Goose collections and by anthologies: among those highly recommended would be Tomie dePaola's *Tomie dePaola's Book Of Poems*[24], Caroline Royds's *Read Me A Poem*[25], Jill Bennett's *Singing In The Sun*[26], Michael Rosen's *A Spider Bought A Bicycle*[27] and Helen Nicoll's *Poems For 7-Year-Olds and Under*[28] (the titles are in ascending order of suitability for age). In the last ten years or so, however, far more individually recognised voices have emerged.

Charles Causley's poems in *Early In The Morning*[29] are the most musical (in fact the hardback version has various of them set to music) and the whole book is a delightful mixture of lyrics, poems so close to nursery rhymes it is difficult to believe we have not known them for ever, and nonsense verse. The opening poem sets the standard for the volume

> *Early in the morning*
> *The water hits the rocks,*
> *The birds are making noises*
> *Like old alarum clocks.*

'In My Garden'

> *In my garden*
> *Grows a tree*
> *Dances day*
> *And night for me*

is surely a half-forgotten nursery rhyme, or a version from Lorca, or ... Who knows, except that it is utterly distinctive!

> *I love my darling tractor,*
> *I love its merry din,*
> *Its muscles made of iron and steel,*
> *Its red and yellow skin*

is born out of Playschool and the reception class and an immense sense of fun.

Michael Rosen's *You Can't Catch Me*[30] –

> *This is the hand*
> *that touched the frost*
> *that froze my tongue*
> *and made it numb –*

is far more up to date in tone, mixing dramatic speech verse with hilarious rhymes and poems that rely on half rather than full rhyme for their effect.

John Agard's *I Din Do Nuttin*[3] contains small poems about little incidents in Dilroy's life:

> *Buying new shoes*
> *takes so long.*
> *When the colour is right*
> *the size is wrong.*

Grace Nichols' *Come On Into My Tropical Garden*[2] is the perfect volume for the child moving from younger to junior-orientated verse, full of exotic settings (Guyana) and recognisable characters, Moody Mister Sometimish and the disciplinarian Ma Bella, 'the fastest belt in town', until she lashes herself by accident. Nichols' poems cannot be recommended too highly for their varied form, the vigour with which she approaches serious and comic subjects alike and for her command of rhyme and rhythm. Nichols and Agard have jointly produced *No Hickory No Dickory No Dock*[1], a collection of Caribbean nursery rhymes

> *Wasn't me*
> *Wasn't me*
> *said the little mouse*
> *I didn't run up no clock*

in which the Caribbean speech rhythms are perfectly captured on the page and the old rhymes reinterpreted in ways that are modern but never silly.

THE MIDDLE RANGE, 8 TO 12

The publication of Charles Causley's *Figgie Hobbin* in 1970 has already been mentioned as a watershed in the history of poetry for children. Causley came to children's writing with a formidable reputation as a writer for adults, chiefly of ballads. The transition was an effortless one, indeed his poems for children sit seamlessly in his *Collected Poems*[31] – personally I would argue that his children's poems are the best of his work.

The ballad form has since the nineteenth century generally been used for purely comic and often slapstick purposes, but

Causley brings to it a seriousness and weight close to that of the original Border Ballad singers, combined with a comic genius and purist literary attitude that believes every word should count, that every rhyme, every stress should have its purpose. His natural style is simple and clear, his diction spare and simple, the sound of his verse sonorous. Many of the poems tell stories, clearly, succinctly, poignantly and he uses every resource in the language to tell them. See how in the opening stanza of 'My Mother Saw A Dancing Bear' he uses the partial rhyme bear/bar to bind the verse together, and how in the second line he uses the natural rhythms of speech to counterpoint the metre the readers expect:

> *My mother saw a dancing bear*
> *By the schoolyard, a day in June.*
> *The keeper stood with chain and bar*
> *And whistle-pipe, and played a tune.*

Figgie Hobbin is one of those miraculous volumes, that perfect moment in a writer's career when everything seems to come together, a book no childhood should be without. Causley is also a marvellous writer of nonsense verse –

> *My son Sam was a banjo man,*
> *His brothers played the spoons,*
> *Willie Waley played the ukelele*
> *And his sister sang the tunes* –

both in *Figgie Hobbin* and in *Early In The Morning*. His *The Tail Of The Trinosaur*[32], an illustrated story poem of over a hundred pages, is also to be recommended as are his anthologies such as *The Puffin Book Of Magic Verse*[33] and *The Puffin Book Of Salt-Sea Verse*[34].

Roger McGough's style in *Sky In The Pie*[35] is more evidently modern than Causley's (Causley with his obvious strong links to nineteenth-century verse and before is in a way an unlikely figure to proclaim as the dawning of a new age in children's poetry) but McGough shares Causley's ability to excite and satisfy both children and exacting adult readers (surely a basic test for a poem's value both as verse for adults and verse for children). Both are traditionalists in that they use rhyme, regular metre, strong subjects to identify with, stirring emotions and vivid imagery, but McGough in this volume (though not always in his other works for children) adds a special tongue-in-cheek quality, a kind of mania which the writer is always in charge of. McGough not only manipulates language with puns (often deliberately terrible), parodies and *doubles entendres*, but also manipulates his subjects, constantly reversing the reader's expectations. A fine example of this is the mock ballad, 'Tell Me Why', ('Daddy will you tell me why,/ There are no battleships in the sky?') in which the movement is from the apparently flippant to the deadly serious:

> *Daddy will you tell me when*
> *Little boys grow into men?*
> *Some never do that's why they fight*
> *Now kiss me, let me hold you tight*
>
> *For in the morning I must go*
> *To join my regiment and so*
> *For Queen and country bravely die*
> *Son, oh son, please tell me why?*

Note the way McGough not only turns the announced subject of the poem and its tone on its head, but also effortlessly breaks the reader's expectation of form, running on the sentence from one verse to the next and continuing the father's voice when you would have expected the child's. McGough is expert at saying the sad in a memorably funny way, whether the subject is something as tragic as in 'Tell Me Why' or a lament for the passing away of the Mersey ferries;

> *No more ferries*
> *No more river trips*
> *No more dreams*
> *on little ships*

Sky In The Pie is, like *Figgie Hobbin*, another of those books that the junior school child should not be without and is also a book that ought, at some point, to be read straight through as each poem, though entirely autonomous, leads on into the next: 'Tell Me Why', for example, leads into 'The Leader' ('I wanna be the leader,/I wanna be the leader') into 'Bully Night' ('Bully night,/I do not like,/the company you keep,/The burglars and the bogeymen,/who slink,/while others sleep').

McGough and Michael Rosen combined forces to produce the
1979 volume *You Tell Me.*[36] McGough's poems come from
various adult collections whereas Rosen's are all originals. The
collection is a lively one and deserves to be read (and often
best read aloud) for poems such as 'Nooligan' ('I'm a
nooligan,/don't give a toss,/in our class,/I'm the boss,/well,
one of them'), 'First Day At School' ('A millionbillionwillion
miles from home,/Waiting for the bell to go. (To go where?)')
by McGough or 'Going Through The Old Photos' ('Who's
that?/That's your Auntie Mabel,/and that's me,/under the
table') and 'Chivvy' ('Grown-ups say things like:/Speak up/
Don't talk with your mouth full,/Don't stare/Don't point/
Don't pick your nose') by Rosen. It will be apparent that while
both poets are irreverent, McGough's work is much more
structured and, dare one say it, literary, while Rosen's is
distinctly throwaway. Rosen's poems (best seen in *Quick, Let's
Get Out Of Here*[8]) appeal to children from nursery age to the
most hardened junior (they often enjoy the same poem).
Unfortunately his monologues, usually in the freest of free
verse, even for those who use his poems frequently (*Quick,
Let's Get Out Of Here* is a supply teacher's dream) can seem flat
and uninviting on the page, the words thrown there almost at
random with little reason for lines ending where they do.
Aloud, however, they work marvellously and their themes,
exploring the boundaries between the adult and child worlds
where so many niggles and conflicts occur, have deeply
influenced the subjects of verse for children in the last few
years: you hear Rosen's voice again and again in anthologies
and individual collections from the eighties. John Rowe
Townsend called the wave of child-centred poetry of the late
seventies 'urchin verse' and the majority of collections since,
with few exceptions, have been for much the same TV-
watching, child-in-school audience. Rosen, it should be added,
is an anthologist with wide-ranging tastes; see *The Kingfisher
Book Of Children's Poetry*[37] and *A World Of Poetry.*[38]

That the only way to cater for this audience is not with such a
radically unstructed form of poetry is proved by the work of
several poets. Alan Ahlberg's *Please Mrs Butler*[7] is a volume that
sits on many teachers' desks and his subject is usually, and
occasionally one feels over-inevitably, school. If Rosen's poetry
explores the clash between children's awkward aspirations and

adults' cherished expectations, Ahlberg's verse depends on the shared experiences of teachers, parents and children/pupils. No adult in an Ahlberg poem would expect or hope the child to be other than he or she is. His poems are carefully and faultlessly modulated, for example,

> *When we pick teams in the playground*
> *Whatever the game might be,*
> *There's always somebody left till last*
> *And usually it's me.*

Ahlberg's verse (other books by Ahlberg to be recommended include *The Mighty Slide*[39], a collection of stories in verse, and *Heard It In The Playground*[40]) rarely, however, counterpoints rhythm with metre in the way of writers such as Stevenson, Milne, Causley or McGough, nor do his images or flights of ideas shock or charm us as forcefully (his prose works are another matter).

A more ambitious, though more uneven writer – like Ahlberg and Rosen he writes only for children – is Gareth Owen whose books include *Song Of The City*[6], *Salford Road*[41] and *My Granny Is A Sumo Wrestler.*[42] Although Owen's subjects might often have been chosen by Rosen, his writing roots are in traditional verse, with frequent echoes in his earlier poems of Stevenson or Reeves, so that his treatments are entirely different. His children are scruffier and more urban than Rosen's or Ahlberg's, from neglected housing estates and terraces, their lives rooted in an identifiable community, with neighbours, uncles and aunties and grandparents effortlessly evoked. His humour is kind and gentle, with the occasional belly-laugh, and he is excellent on family life and the privacies within it. 'Half Asleep' could almost be by a latter-day Stevenson:

> *Half asleep*
> *And half awake*
> *I drift like a boat*
> *On an empty lake.*
> *And the sounds in the house*
> *And the street that I hear*
> *Though far away sound very clear.*

Owen also writes monologues in free verse: see his typographical masterpiece, 'Typewriting Class', or 'The Commentator', a commentary on a soccer international in the back garden that goes horribly wrong.

OTHER RECOMMENDED POETS FOR THE 8 TO 12 AGE GROUP:

- John Mole's volumes include *Boo To A Goose*[43] and *The Mad Parrot's Countdown.*[44] Many of Mole's best poems for children were actually first published for adults and explore the inexplicable terrors of childhood. His work reminds us like Owen's that there are other ways of organising verse than simple rhyming.
- Brian Patten is best known for *Gargling With Jelly*[45] and is already widely read in schools. Patten is an extremely skilful manipulator of words (he seems to be able to rhyme anything and get away with it). An adult might feel an uneasy relationship between technical virtuosity and a constant impulse to amuse.
- The poems in the American Valerie Worth's *All The Small Poems*[46] quite definitely do not rhyme. Few poems are longer than a page, few lines longer than three or four words. They are excellent models for children writing their own tightly controlled free verse.
- The black American Nikki Giovanni (*Spin A Soft Black Song*[47]) will find an audience all through the primary school. She writes short, spare poems close to speech rhythms and catches children's preoccupations as well as Rosen.
- Russell Hoban's *The Pedalling Man*[48] is written with a family warmth. The poems are conventionally structured, the description of small objects and experiences is done with precision.
- The poem in Jackie Kay's *Two's Company*[49] range from the wildly improbable (a skelf [splinter] helpline) to poems that reflect the collection's title: poems about friendship and its loss or lack, poems about an imaginary friend or living in two households because your parents have split up.

Poetry for older children

There is of course no clear dividing line between the poetry children will enjoy at nine and ten or at eleven and twelve. The poetry that follows is not so much more *difficult* (though it occasionally is – it sometimes requires a more trained response to language and occasionally a wider breadth of experience than you would expect in a junior child) as *different*.

Philip Gross's first books were for adults, but on the evidence so far his work for children is likely to be more enduring. *Manifold Manor*[50] is a series of connected poems about an old house haunted by ghosts and voices from the past. Three pages of notes finish the volume and for anyone, child or adult, interested in poetic form and the possibilities of extending their technique, they are a must. Gross is innovative technically, though he never uses his facility at playing with form self-consciously. In 'The Cry-by-night' the rhymes never quite get there (Gross suggests the effect is like playing notes a semi-tone apart):

> *Where is she? You* must *know. Down quiet*
> *corridors, up stairs, you follow listening*
> *at every door, nearly there, never quite.*

The All-Nite Café[51], his second and most recent volume, is probably more accessible for less experienced readers, with a wider range of subjects and more poems directly about children's experiences. The technical interest, though, is still there. See, for example, 'Multi Storey' which uses the stress on the last word of each stanza to enhance the creepiness of the experience:

> *'Level 13. Don't forget. By the car,'*
> *they said. 'Don't be late.'*
> *But you are.*
>
> *You punch the buttons one by one*
> *No hum. The lift is dead.*
> *So you run …*

Ted Hughes's *Meet My Folks!*[22] has already been mentioned as a book more enjoyable for its individual poems than as a

whole. This was early Hughes for children. His books since
have been much more like his adult work. This is Hughes's
great strength as a writer for children; he rarely writes
deliberately for them. He gives them the whole experience of
his ability as a writer, ignoring the preconceptions we may
have as adults about the way we think he should write for
them.

What Is The Truth?[52] is a long book with some very long poems
printed in double columns and with a linking prose narrative:
God and his Son have come to earth and question villagers
about the animals they know best. The poems are in a variety
of forms, some free verse, some using different rhyme
schemes. The villagers don't share the same views of the
animals so that, for example, you get the farmer's son's
version, the poacher's and the farmer's. *Moon-bells*[53] is for
slightly older children: there are several rather baffling poems
about moon-creatures, but the rest is superb mainstream
Hughes. You will probably already know 'Amulet', a poem that
sometimes causes adults problems, but which children at even
quite a young age take to when they understand the circular
nature of the poem, the association of ideas that pulls the
poem forward, the idea of Oneness: it is a poem that will get
them writing too.

> *Inside the wolf's fang, the mountain of heather.*
> *Inside the mountain of heather, the wolf's fur.*
> *Inside the wolf's fur, the ragged forest.*
> *Inside the ragged forest, the wolf's foot.*

Season Songs[9], however, is like *Figgie Hobbin* and *Sky In The Pie*, a
book that no child should be deprived of. When it was
published there were doubts whether this was a children's or
an adult's book (there are no illustrations), but it is actually a
book for both adults and children, and many of the poems will
be appreciated by quite young children. Rhyme is just one of
many devices Hughes uses to organise his poems. In 'Leaves', a
version of 'Who Killed Cock Robin', the repetition of the first
and last lines of each stanza as well as the rhyme pulls the
poem forward:

Who'll be their parson?
Me, says the Crow, for it is well-known
I study the bible right down to the bone.
I'll be their parson.

In 'The Warm And The Cold' rhyme is used conventionally:

Freezing dusk is closing
   Like a slow trap of steel
On trees and roads and hills and all
   That can no longer feel.

though you might consider the slow movement of the rhythm, which almost hampers the poem's progress forward, together with the almost searingly vivid imagery, is the most striking feature of the poetry. The last lines,

Such a frost
The flimsy moon
Has lost her wits.

A star falls.

The sweating farmers
Turn in their sleep
Like oxen on spits.

are not only quintissentially English (Hughes's poetry like Causley's always links out to the traditions of poetry we hope children will be reading as adults) but also like the distillation of several haiku. If rhyme is at bottom not a prerequisite for a piece of writing being a poem but one of many organisational devices a poet has at his command, then the fact that you hardly notice whether the poems in this volume are rhymed or not can only be a compliment as Hughes in 'Spring Nature Notes' combines the sublime and the ridiculous in a series of delicate images.

With arms swinging, a tremendous skater
On the flimsy ice of space,
The earth leans into its curve —

Thrilled to the core, some flies have waded out
An inch onto my window, to stand on the sky
And try their buzz.

With *Season Songs* we have reached the point where publishers start to talk about writing for teenagers and although the poetry may be no more difficult, the subjects are less likely to be of interest to younger children. In this field James Berry's *When I Dance*[4] has the same stature as *Figgie Hobbin*[13] or the Hughes volume, and Rosen (*When Did You Last Wash Your Feet?*[54]), Gowar (*So Far So Good*[55]) and Michael Gizzie (*Deep Holy Joe And The Ballad Of The Band*[56]) have also written volumes that can be highly recommended.

I have mentioned throughout the poet as anthologist, Causley and Rosen in particular. Ted Hughes and Seamus Heaney's *The Rattle Bag*[57] is the ideal introduction for teenagers to adult poetry, but the doyen of anthologists is Anne Harvey whose emphasis is upon British twentieth-century writing. The poems she chooses are deeply felt, carefully observed and well constructed. Her anthologies include *Faces In A Crowd*[58], *In Time Of War*[59], *Occasions*[60] and *Six Of The Best*[61], a volume particularly to be recommended for its choices from Phoebe Hesketh, Russell Hoban and, above all, Alan Brownjohn, whose poems for children have not been mentioned previously but which deserve to be far more widely known.

ℛEFERENCES

1. Agard, J. and Nichols, G. (1991) *No Hickory No Dickory No Dock*. London: Viking
2. Nichols, G. (1988) *Come On Into My Tropical Garden*. London: Black
3. Agard, J. (1983) *I Din Do Nuttin*. London: Mammoth
4. Berry, J. (1988) *When I Dance*. London: Hamish Hamilton
5. Stevenson, R.L. (1885) *A Child's Garden Of Verses*. Harmondsworth: Puffin 1952
6. Owen, G. (1985) *Song Of The City*. London: Young Lion
7. Ahlberg, A. (1983) *Please Mrs Butler*. London: Viking
8. Rosen, M. (1983) *Quick, Let's Get Out Of Here*. London: Deutsch
9. Hughes, T (1976) *Season Songs*. London: Faber
10. Opie, I. and Opie, P. (1973) *The Oxford Book Of Children's Verse*. Oxford: Oxford University Press
11. Graham, E. (1958) *A Puffin Quartet of Poets*. Harmondsworth: Puffin

12. Reeves, J. (1973) *Complete Poems For Children.* London: Heinemann
13. Causley, C. (1970) *Figgie Hobbin.* London: Viking
14. Rossetti, C. (1872) *Sing-Song.* USA: Dover Thrift 1994
15. Rossetti, C. (1862) *Goblin Market.* USA: Dover 1969
16. de la Mare, W. (1944) *Collected Rhymes and Verses.* London: Faber
17. Belloc, H. (1940) *Selected Cautionary Tales.* London: Puffin
18. Nash, O. (1979) *Custard And Company.* London: Puffin Books
19. Lear, (1845) *A Book Of Nonsense.* London: Dent 1992
20. Peake, M. (1944) *Rhymes Without Reason.* London: Methuen
21. Eliot, T.S. (1939) *Old Possum's Book Of Practical Cats.* London: Faber
22. Hughes, T. (1961) *Meet My Folks!* London: Faber
23. Milne, A.A. (1924) *When We Were Very Young.* London: Methuen
24. dePaola, T. (1989) *Tomie dePaola's Book Of Poems.* London: Methuen
25. Royds, C. (1987) *Read Me A Poem.* London: Kingfisher
26. Bennett, J. (1988) *Singing In The Sun.* London: Viking
27. Rosen, M. (1987) *A Spider Bought A Bicycle.* London: Kingfisher
28. Nicoll, H. (1983) *Poems For 7-Year-Olds And Under.* London: Viking
29. Causley, C. (1986) *Early In The Morning.* London: Viking
30. Rosen, M. (1981) *You Can't Catch Me.* London: Deutsch
31. Causley, C. (1992) *Collected Poems.* London: Macmillan London Ltd
32. Causley, C. (1973) *The Tail Of The Trinosaur.* London: Viking
33. Causley, C. (1974) *The Puffin Book Of Magic Verse.* London: Viking
34. Causley, C. (1978) *The Puffin Book Of Salt-Sea Verse.* London: Viking
35. McGough, R. (1984) *Sky In The Pie.* London: Viking
36. McGough, R. and Rosen, M. (1979) *You Tell Me.* London: Viking
37. Rosen, M. (1985) *The Kingfisher Book Of Children's Poetry.* London: Kingfisher
38. Rosen, M. (1991) *A World Of Poetry.* London: Kingfisher
39. Ahlberg, A. (1988) *The Mighty Slide.* London: Viking
40. Ahlberg, A. (1990) *Heard It In The Playground.* London: Viking

41. Owen, G. (1979) *Salford Road.* London: Kestrel
42. Owen, G. (1994) *My Granny Is A Sumo Wrestler.* London: Young Lion
43. Mole, J. (1987) *Boo To A Goose.* Calstock, Cornwall: Peterloo Poets
44. Mole, J. (1990) *The Mad Parrot's Countdown.* Calstock, Cornwall: Peterloo Poets
45. Patten, B. (1985) *Gargling With Jelly.* London: Viking
46. Worth, V. (1987) *All The Small Poems.* London: Faber
47. Giovanni, N. (1971) *Spin A Soft Sad Song.* New York: Farrar, Strauss and Giroux
48. Hoban, R. (1968) *The Pedalling Man.* London: Heineman
49. Kay, J. (1992) *Two's Company.* London: Blackie
50. Gross, P. (1989) *Manifold Manor.* London: Faber
51. Gross, P. (1993) *The All-Nite Café.* London: Faber
52. Hughes, T. (1984) *What Is The Truth?* London: Faber
53. Hughes, T. (1978) *Moon-bells.* London: Chatto and Windus
54. Rosen, M. (1986) *When Did You Last Wash Your Feet?* London: Deutsch
55. Gowar, M. (1986) *So Far So Good.* London: Puffin Plus
56. Gizzie, M. (1990) *Deep Holy Joe And The Ballad Of The Band.* London: Walker
57. Hughes, T. and Heaney, S. (1982) *The Rattle Bag.* London: Faber
58. Harvey, A. (1990) *Faces In A Crowd.* London: Viking
59. Harvey, A. (1987) *In Time Of War.* London: Blackie
60. Harvey, A. (1990) *Occasions.* London: Blackie
61. Harvey, A. (1989) *Six Of The Best.* London: Puffin

7

USING RHYME WITH SPECIAL NEEDS CHILDREN

Frances James

> *Humpty Dumpty sat on a log*
> *Humpty Dumpty saw a big frog.*

As a teacher involved in the education of children with a range of learning difficulties, I have always been very conscious of those children who encounter difficulty in acquiring the skills that are necessary to be a fluent and accurate reader. Marilyn Jager Adams[1] has identified four main processors which are essential to the reading process (see figure 7.1). These are the orthographic processor, which relates to the children's ability to recognise words by sight, the meaning and contextual

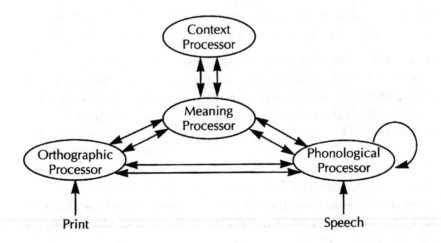

FIGURE 7.1. *The four main processors essential to the reading process.*

processors, which allow children to use their understanding of words and grammar to construct meaning from the text, and the phonological processor which relates the sound system in language to the written representations. Children need to develop the use of all these processors and approaches to the teaching of reading should reflect this.

The use of the phonological processor is frequently the aspect of reading that children with literacy difficulties find most challenging. There is increasing evidence, for example from Valerie Muter[2], that children with specific learning difficulties have particular difficulty with the phonological components of reading. One of the characteristics of a poor reader is that they rely too heavily on context and 'guessing' and they do not have the necessary skills to decode new words when they encounter them. Poor phonological skills, undoubtedly, have an impact on the child's spelling too.

Teaching children with literacy difficulties is, in many ways, a constant search for approaches which will be meaningful and successful for the child, building on their existing knowledge to take them towards the goal of fluent reading. Teaching phonics, in such a way, has long been a challenge. My personal teaching experience has shown that pupils with literacy difficulties find the identification and use of individual phonemes (the smallest sound units in speech) difficult, particularly the vowel sounds. I have also been concerned that teaching phonics could be a dull activity which I, certainly, found difficult to present in an exciting and meaningful way.

With these things in mind I was constantly searching for suggestions from others' teaching practice and research evidence which would indicate ways in which children with literacy difficulties could be taught the essential phonic building blocks. The book that seemed to offer constructive and positive ways forward was *Children's Reading Difficulties* by Peter Bryant and Lynette Bradley.[3] In this book Bryant and Bradley identified the importance of children's ability to recognise rhyme and alliteration in speech and how this has an impact on their reading ability. They noted how children's knowledge of nursery rhymes was a predictor of later reading skills. There is a description of an intervention with pupils, who had been identified as having poor literacy skills, in which they were taught, with plastic letters, the relationship between what they heard in words and the spelling patterns in word families. These children achieved better reading levels than matched controls. The control group had similar amounts of teaching time but this concentrated on different aspects of language development. The experimental group also fared better than another control group which had explored the oral features of words but did not use the plastic letters to make the connection with spelling features.

The word of Bryant and Bradley had been developed further by Bryant and Goswami[4] and Goswami.[5] They propose that there is a developmental strand to children's growing appreciation of sounds; the children recognise rhyme, rime and onset and then, with this knowledge, can break the larger sound units into the individual phonemes. Usha Goswami has introduced teachers to the importance of children's sense of analogy, relating their knowledge of sounds to the spelling patterns in words.

All this work offered ways of developing teaching approaches and curriculum materials to address difficulties that children encounter when learning to read. I am fortunate to work with a team of advisory teachers and colleagues in schools who recognise the value of exploring new techniques to tackle children's difficulties and, with the support of the LEA, we undertook a project to investigate ways of translating the exciting research findings into classroom practice, with a specific emphasis on early identification and intervention. We are aware that we are not the only ones to undertake such work and that very interesting projects have been initiated by others, including Lyn Layton and her colleagues, based at Birmingham University.

THE PROJECT DESIGN

Four nurseries were selected to be involved in the project. It was decided that the target group of children would be all those who had one term left in nursery. Two nurseries were provided with ideas for developing children's general language skills and the other two with curriculum ideas that promoted children's appreciation of rhyme. These ideas had

been developed in an initial project by a highly skilled teacher.
The curriculum ideas were explicitly used during the children's
last term in nursery and in their first term of reception class.
All the children were assessed before the interventions, using a
range of measures, and again at the end of the two terms. The
children are still being tracked to see if there are many marked
differences in their reading and spelling performances. We
recognise that there are many variables and possible
contamination, and the project was not designed as 'pure'
research. The overall aim was to develop curriculum and
assessment approaches that would be useful for teachers. The
developments arising from this project and subsequent work
are described below.

ASSESSMENT

The cornerstone of any good curriculum intervention,
particularly for pupils with special educational needs, is clear
assessment information. Good assessment information should
also allow teachers to identify pupils who are 'at risk' and
facilitate early intervention.

In the project certain well-established standardised assessments
were used – The British Picture Vocabulary Scale (BPVS) and
the British Ability Scales single word reading test – but we
wished to develop criterion referenced assessments which
would tap the children's developing phonological knowledge.

Bryant and Bradley[3] had noted the predictive nature of
children's knowledge of nursery rhymes. Discussion with
teachers suggested that children were coming to school without
the experience and knowledge of nursery rhymes that was,
perhaps, evident in the past. We felt that it was important to
gauge the children's knowledge of nursery rhymes. In the first
stage of the project children were asked to recite three nursery
rhymes. In recognition of the local variation in children's
knowledge of nursery rhymes, an informal survey was
conducted to find the most commonly known nursery rhymes.
The results of this survey suggested that 'Baa, Baa, Black
Sheep', 'Humpty Dumpty' and 'Jack and Jill' were the most
popular and so the children were asked to recite these. They
were also asked if they wanted to say any other rhymes, just in
case they didn't know the target rhymes.

We originally noted every error that the children made but this proved to be a cumbersome method of recording. We concluded that the important feature of the children's recital was whether they knew the rhyming pairs of words and so a scoring sheet was devised that recorded each pair that the child successfully remembered; for example fall-wall, men-again. (This scoring method highlighted that, as Usha Goswami pointed out Chapter 4, many of the 'rhyming' pairs in nursery rhymes are not actually true rhymes.) A further amendment was made once we had tried this approach. Most of the children did not know the second verse of 'Jack and Jill' and so 'Twinkle, Twinkle Little Star' was substituted. This allowed the children to score a maximum of ten correct 'rhyming' pairs. Use of the approach demonstrated that nursery aged children have varying knowledge of the most common nursery rhymes. Teachers noted that there was a correlation between those children who had poor nursery rhyme knowledge and general delay of language development.

We wanted to determine which children were able to identify words that rhyme and those that share the same initial sound. Lynette Bradley[6] has devised the 'Oddity Task' which addresses these skills. In the task the teacher says four words; for example 'hat, mat, fan, cat' and the child is asked to identify the odd one out. There are three conditions, the first in which the last sound is different (as in the example given), in the second the middle sound differs and in the third condition the first sound is different. This assessment is designed for children of a similar age to our target group but when we used it to assess the children, all of them found it very difficult. Considerable debate took place about why this could be and several suggestions were made. Observations suggested that some children had difficulty remembering the four words and so their memory restricted their performance; in other cases the children had difficulty understanding the concept of 'odd one out' and, thus, did not comprehend the nature of the task as a whole.

It was felt to be important to develop a different way of assessing the children's recognition of rhyme and alliteration that avoided a load on the children's short-term memory and the concept of odd one out. The solution which suggested itself was a picture matching task. Pictures of four common objects were drawn on a board. The child was asked to name the objects. She or he was then shown another picture which rhymes with one of the four pictures and was asked to place it on top of the picture with which it rhymes. A similar task was designed to assess the children's appreciation of alliteration.

At Hull University, Chris Singleton is developing a computer based bank of assessment tasks which endeavour to identify young children who may have literacy difficulties. We are very grateful to Dr Singleton for the interest he has shown in our work. The rhyme matching task has been incorporated into the computer assessment suite. The research team in Hull have conducted an extensive initial pilot and the results are very encouraging; 80 per cent of children who do eventually manifest reading difficulties were correctly identified using the eight elements of the computer assessment, including the rhyme matching task.

There is considerable debate about whether children with literacy difficulties have problems with phonological processing overall or whether they have difficulties with specific aspects. Certain researchers have suggested that phonological memory is the area that causes particular problems. In recognition of this we incorporated a simple digit span test in the assessment materials to explore the children's short-term auditory memory. This requires children to repeat sequences of numbers of increasing length; they are asked to repeat the numbers in the same order in one condition and in reverse order in the other condition.

As the work progresses additions have been made to the assessment materials. Susan Gavarcole, of Lancaster University, has devised a test which requires children to repeat nonsense words of differing syllabic lengths. This task involves several aspects of phonological processing, the ability to distinguish certain sounds, to make analogies with 'proper' words, to reproduce sounds and, of course, auditory short-term memory. This has proved to be a valuable and informative assessment.

We are now using all the assessment materials with older children about whom teachers have expressed concern. Some of these children have begun to develop more sophisticated phonic skills and, to recognise this, a sheet for recording children's knowledge of letter sounds has been included, as has a recording sheet for letter names.

CURRICULUM

We wished to construct a range of curriculum activities that had a broad developmental framework which reflected the growing research evidence and which allowed teachers to differentiate activities in recognition of children's different abilities, interests and skills. The framework fell into four main stages:

- general auditory awareness – listening skills, appreciation of rhythm, knowledge of nursery rhymes, etc.;
- recognition of words that rhyme orally;
- recognition of words that rhyme and share the same spelling pattern;
- development of the sense of analogy through the use of plastic letters.

Stage 1

The importance of listening skills in developing children's concepts, skills and knowledge across the curriculum is indisputable and it has, obviously, particular relevance for the development of specific auditory skills. Teachers report that their informal observations suggest that children's listening skills are, often, not as well developed as one would wish when they join school. Certain reasons for this have been put forward. Children receive much of their information visually and the dominance of television and computer games contribute to this. It is possible to receive most of the key information from the television by following the pictures and not paying close attention to the spoken word. Busy lives, in all families, may well be reducing the opportunities for discussion and conversation. Oral traditions, such as story-telling and nursery rhymes, are not as current as they were.

Owing to these observations we considered it important to include a range of activities that emphasised listening. These included games such as 'Simon Says', 'Chinese Whispers' and an aural version of 'Kim's Game' and asking children to follow and remember increasingly complex instructions and messages. Teachers were encouraged to use commercially produced tapes of animal and environmental sounds for the children to identify and recall. These was also a rich diet of story-telling and use of story tapes.

Another important aspect of the work, at this stage, was developing children's appreciation of rhythm and sound. The aim of this was to sensitise children to the rhythm of speech and, particularly, within words. Spoken speech is a stream of sound and listeners need to develop an acuity to the rhythm of speech to identify individual words. (As their reading develops, the children recognise that the individual words they hear are identified by spaces between them on the page.) When children recognise rhythm in words they will begin to recognise syllables, a very important skill, and then the phonological units within syllables, at first the onset and rime and then the phonemes.

One way of developing children's sense of rhythm is through music and dance. Suggestions for using percussion instruments were included, as were a range of dance and movement activities. The children were encouraged to clap their names and also words that had different rhythmic patterns. Some teachers developed dance patterns to accompany these rhythms.

Perhaps the strongest thread throughout stage 1 was the emphasis on teaching children rhymes of all types. These included not only traditional nursery rhymes but also action rhymes (for example 'Jelly on the Plate') number rhymes and action rhymes ('Round and round the garden'). Teachers incorporated contemporary rhymes, including advertising jingles, into the work and rhymes from different cultures. As the original assessments suggested many of the children had limited knowledge of nursery rhymes. Some of the assessments surprised the teachers as they thought the children knew the common nursery rhymes but found that the children were mouthing certain lines of the rhymes. This emphasised the importance of checking that all children truly knew the words. Instead of reciting the rhymes as a class the teachers occasionally asked small groups or individuals to recite them. Children took it in turns to say one line at a time. A useful way of assessing the children's knowledge was by using a tape recorder to record individual children. Tape recorded collections were made to complement the class books of nursery rhymes.

Children drew pictures from their favourite rhymes which were collated into class books. Small groups of children acted out the stories from different rhymes and these were performed to the whole class and occasionally videoed. Schools involved parents by asking them for nursery rhymes which they knew when they were at school. Grandparents and members of the extended family also volunteered to share rhymes from their youth. As the Opies'[8] respected work records, there are some fascinating regional variations in rhymes (see also Georgina Boyes' chapter which follows). Playground rhymes have some of the most interesting variations. Teachers taught the children a range of playground rhymes and games. Staff supervising play and dinner times were asked to join in with the children and encourage these activities. These can be a positive side-effect of encouraging playground rhymes. Children who are purposively occupied at playtimes are less likely to engage in poor behaviour. There are, of course, a number of other benefits from this work; the number rhymes feed into children's growing knowledge about number in general. All the activities have a positive effect on the children's social skills and their general language development. We noted that the children who experienced the rhyme curriculum tended to extend their overall receptive language skills, as measured by the BPVS, more than the control group.

Stage 2

The focus of this stage was to enhance the children's recognition of words that rhyme and alliterate. All the work was oral and so the words used did not have to share the same spelling pattern. The children's aural recognition of similarities and differences within words was the teaching target.

Many of the activities built on the children's knowledge of nursery rhymes and rhymes in general. Teachers began to draw the children's attention to the words that rhymed in nursery rhymes, asking the children to supply missing words; for example 'Jack and ..., Went up the ...'. The children were asked if they noticed anything about the words. The importance of introducing the correct terminology to the children was emphasised; words such as *rhyme, sound* and *begin.* (Many children with special educational needs encounter additional difficulties because they do not understand the words that are associated with aspects of their learning.) As the example shows at the beginning of this chapter, new versions of traditional nursery rhymes were created with the children: 'Humpty Dumpty sat on a chair/hill/train/log/floor, Humpty Dumpty saw a ....'. Children filled in the missing words appropriately, including those children who could not articulate why the words were appropriate. Children illustrated the new versions of the rhymes.

Rhyming tables or displays were created in the classrooms. Adults and children brought in objects that rhymed with a key word. In other weeks the display might focus on objects that begin with the same letter because the importance of alliteration (in other words, the onset of syllables) was stressed at this stage too. Children were taught tongue twisters and then developed their own alliterative phrases using their own names.

Great use was made of pictures of objects that rhyme and also those that begin with the same initial sound. These were used for games of snap, bingo, for making sets and pairs. In the initial project the teacher made puppets with names like Dan, Ann and Sid. The children used the puppets to collect pictures of objects that 'belonged' to the puppet. Worksheets were developed; for example there are several containers (pot, can, bag, tin) which have rhyming potential and the children were asked to draw rhyming objects in the correct container. In an extension of the project one teacher made cards with laces and the children were required to join the rhyming pictures.

Teachers used informal opportunities to reinforce the concepts of rhyme and alliteration and it became an integral part of the school or nursery day. One of the support staff visited a school involved in the project and was asked her name. When she said that her name was Pat, the child replied 'That rhymes with cat!'.

Stage 3

The next stage was to introduce children to the written representations of the words and to begin to draw their attention to the patterns in the words. It was important at this stage that words chosen for the activity did share spelling patterns; for example chair and stair and not chair and bear.

Many of the activities were the same as stage 2 but now words were written to go with the pictures. For some children, who were beginning to develop faster, word recognition cards were used which just had the word written on. As with all teaching activities it was important to differentiate and not to hold back children who were advancing well. Another important strand was to draw children's attention to words which shared the same spelling patterns in books. As Marilyn Jager Adams[1] notes, the most effective teaching of reading is when systematic code instruction takes place in the context of meaningful text. Big books proved very useful for this purpose.

Children were encouraged to write and copy short phrases which contained rhyming or alliterative words. In one school, in a second phase of the project, a teacher asked the children to paint pictures of animals after generating rhyming phrases; a wonderful collection resulted of a moose on the loose, a frog on a log, a cat in the hat, etc. Similar collections were made into class books. Teachers found that they could link rhymes and poems into general class topics.

Stage 4

This is the stage that Bryant and Bradley[3] found to be central to the sustained progress that the children in their study made. It is when children formalise the link (or analogy) between their knowledge of the sounds of words and the written pattern. It requires the teacher to work with individual children, something which can be hard to arrange in a busy classroom, but the short time it takes pays great dividends. The child is asked make a regular word, such as 'cat', with plastic letters. The teacher asks the child to make a rhyming word, for example 'hat'. In many cases the child will start afresh seeking the letters h, a and t. The temptation is to tell the child that they only need to change one letter but the teacher lets them continue with the individual letters. Another rhyming word is chosen and this continues until the child realises that there is a more economic way of tackling the task and that the existing letters can be used. It is at this point that the teacher intervenes and consolidates the child's own discovery. It is important, particularly with children who have learning difficulties, to encourage them to articulate their discovery. If a child describes what they have learnt the chances of them remembering it are increased.

Once the child has had this experience there should be plenty of opportunities for them to consolidate the knowledge. There is not such a need for intensive teacher involvement because the children can work in groups discovering which word families have the most members, using plastic letters or writing them. Teachers have made 'flip books' in which rimes are constant but by turning pages you see different onsets; the children have to record the words that can be made in this way. There are other ways of presenting this, using spinners, dominoes, cards, etc.

As the children developed a more sophisticated appreciation of phonological features in words, teachers began to refine this knowledge further by helping the children to recognise individual phonemes. It has been observed that children, especially those with learning difficulties, find it hard to isolate individual vowel sounds and so it remains profitable to associate the vowel sounds with the following consonant, within the syllable, for example -im.

Throughout all this work teachers exposed the children to a wide range of rhyme and poetry. Story times included rhyming stories, poetry, rhymes and jingles. This reinforced the phonological work and provided a broad and rich literary environment for all pupils.

All the ideas that were developed in this project and in the pilot were collated into a 'Rhyme' booklet[9] which was distributed to all Suffolk schools.

FURTHER DEVELOPMENTS

As I have indicated the work from this project has been taken up as the basis of other projects. In one group of schools it was decided to adapt the materials to use with Y3 and 4 children who were identified, by their teachers, as encountering literacy difficulties. These children were assessed using the materials developed in the original project and their reading ages were measured.

Many of the children were unable to recognise rhyme and alliteration and their knowledge of nursery rhymes was poor. It was felt that nursery rhymes were not necessarily appropriate for these older children and so teachers used rhymes from the best of traditional and contemporary children's literature to introduce the concept of rhyme at a more age-appropriate level. Another feature of the children's knowledge was a confusion between letter names and sounds. This provided another clear teaching target when introducing onsets to certain children. There was an emphasis on using the information gleaned from the initial assessment to plan specific interventions for individual children, differentiating the tasks and teacher intervention.

Other tasks were introduced to supplement the materials. As some of the children had rudimentary writing skills, activities such as simple crosswords, word searches and cloze exercises were used. Rhyme was used in some very imaginative cross-curricular ways. In one school a geography task (orienteering around the school grounds) was achieved by children finding their destinations by using rhyming clues. A technology task required the children to design a game for their peers which had a rhyming element. Many of the schools used ancillary or parental support to deliver, particularly, the oral aspects of the work.

The intensive intervention lasted for only six weeks. To reassess children using standardised tests after such a short time is notoriously unreliable but there were indications that most had made gains in their reading ages. All but one child, from a total cohort of approximately 35, had made gains on the criterion referenced assessments – recognition of rhyme, alliteration, knowledge of letter names and sounds and the children's ability to generate words from the same word family.

REFLECTIONS ON THE PROJECTS

We are conducting an overall quantitative analysis of the children's progress and there are clear indications that the children, in all phases in the project, made progress in their learning as measured by standardised and criterion referenced assessments. This is obviously very important but so are the qualitative evaluation made by the teachers and the children.

One of the aims of the work was to develop assessment and curriculum materials that could be used as part of normal primary classroom practice. Teachers felt that this had been achieved and many of the activities were extensions of what was part of the early years' curriculum. The activities fit well with the requirements of the new National Curriculum orders for English, which will guarantee their continuing place in teachers' approach to developing children's reading skills. Another important criterion for evaluating the success of the materials was that they were enjoyable; it is far easier to teach something well if one can deliver the materials with enthusiasm. Teachers' responses to the materials indicated that they and the children had responded positively to the activities.

The assessment materials were found to be useful but time-consuming to use with all children. It was felt that the full range were applicable for children who were not making the progress that one would hope for. The assessment did, however, provide a developmental framework for children's phonological knowledge which teachers were able to use with all children as they made informal observations of the child's reading behaviour.

For children with literacy difficulties the information from the assessment provides teaching priorities. This is of particular relevance with the introduction of the Code of Practice[10]. Schools are now expected to employ a staged approach to the assessment of children with special educational needs. At stage 1 the class teacher identifies the nature of the child's difficulties and is expected to differentiate teaching approaches to meet the child's needs. At stage 2 the special needs co-ordinator is more involved and, with the class teacher, devises an individual education plan for the child.

A high proportion of children identified as having special educational needs in primary schools have literacy difficulties and frequently these relate to weak phonological skills. The developmental information that the assessment materials provide allow teachers to make clear descriptions of the nature of the child's specific difficulties. The materials and activities are suitable for providing the required differentiated approaches to teaching and, if necessary, the foundation of individual education plans.

The work continues. There are many fascinating projects across the country and these will be used to inform future work. Usha Goswami's work on analogy has much to teach us and we hope to develop some of her ideas through the use of information technology. Chris Singleton's work has tremendous potential for the early identification of pupils with specific learning difficulties and the subsequent strategies used to address the difficulties. It is very exciting: perhaps one of the most exciting facets is that one of the richest literary veins, poetry and nursery rhymes, can be tapped to provide the foundation for helping children with literacy difficulties.

FOOTNOTE

It will be evident from this chapter that it represents the work of many colleagues. It is important to recognise the work of teachers at Edgar Sewter CP School, Northfield St Nicholas CP School, Roman Hill CP School and all the primary schools in South Lowestoft. Members of the Pupil Services team, particularly Ann Kerr, Jane Buckley and Barbara Tyler, have made invaluable contributions. Ann David was responsible for developing many of the initial curriculum activities. We are all grateful for the support of Suffolk LEA, including that of Peter Daw, the County Adviser for English.

—————————— *R*EFERENCES ——————————

1. Adams, M.J. (1990) *Beginning to Read: Thinking and Learning About Print.* Cambridge, Mass.: MIT Press
2. Muter, V. (1994) 'The influence of phonological awareness and letter knowledge on beginning reading and spelling development' in Hulme, C. and Snowling, M. (Eds.) *Reading Development and Dyslexia.* Newcastle-Upon Tyne: Whurr Publishers Ltd.
3. Bryant, P.E. and Bradley, L. (1985) *Children's Reading Problems.* Oxford: Basil Blackwell
4. Goswami, U. and Bryant, P.E. (1990) *Phonological Skills and Learning to Read.* Hove: Lawrence Erlbaum Associates
5. Goswami, U. (1994) 'Reading by Analogy: Theoretical and Practical Perspectives' in Hulme, C. and Snowling, M. (Eds.) *Reading Development and Dyselxia.* Newcastle-Upon-Tyne: Whurr Publishers Ltd.
6. Bradley, L. (1984) *Assessing Reading Difficulties: A Diagnostic and Remedial Approach*, Second edition. London: MacMillan Education
7. Singleton, C. and Thomas, K. (1994) 'Computerised Screening for Dyslexia' in Singleton, C. (Ed.) *Computers and Dyslexia.* Hull: The Dyslexia Computer Resource Centre
8. Opie, I. and Opie, P. (1969) *Children's Games in Street and Playground.* Oxford: Oxford University Press
9. Suffolk County Council (1993) *Rhyme: A Resource for Teachers of Reading*
10. *Code of Practice on the Identification and Assessment of Special Educational Needs.* (1994) UK Central Office of Education.

8

§§

THE LEGACY OF THE WORK OF IONA AND PETER OPIE: THE LORE AND LANGUAGE OF TODAY'S CHILDREN

Georgina Boyes

> *Ip dip doo*
> *Cat's on the loo*
> *Baby's got the chickenpox*
> *Out goes you*[1]

When *The Lore and Language of Schoolchildren*[2] was published in 1959, it made captivating reading. For the first time, the rich diversity and long history of children's play rhymes, beliefs and customs were comprehensively documented. Iona and Peter Opie's research in streets and playgrounds across Britain provided a fascinating revelation of the hidden creativity running through the everyday experience of childhood – deeply appreciated by children themselves, forgotten or undervalued by adults. But their book was more than a lively and accessible account of young people's language and rituals – it also set out a revolutionary new view of children's culture. The Opies convincingly proposed that the rhymes children made for themselves were 'more than playthings', their verses were vivid, constantly renewed art forms, which also functioned as vital social supports amid the jostling life of the school yard. Children, they found, maintained a dynamic oral heritage, which constantly intermixed popular and traditional elements to keep old forms alive and create new ones. History and modernity existed side by side. Riddles first recorded in

1511 were still known by schoolboys in Oxford in the 1950s, York schoolgirls skipped to a variant of a ballad written in 1725 – but they and their contemporaries were equally delighted by riddles about tins of tomatoes and rhymes about Teddy Boys and Popeye. Confounding the pessimists who claimed that folklore was dead and modern children lost in passive consumerism, the Opies triumphantly showed a generation 'rich in language, well-versed in custom', 'which cares for the traditions and entertainments which have been passed down to it'. They revealed that folklore was flourishing in streets and playgrounds throughout Britain, in town and country and across all social classes – 'children with homes and backgrounds as different from each other as mining community and garden suburb share jokes, rhymes and songs which are basically identical'. As literature, cultural study and work of scholarship, therefore, *The Lore and Language of Schoolchildren* was a landmark. But generations have 'tumbled and rhymed' out of school since it first appeared, Gameboys and My Little Pony have replaced Davy Crocket hats, reputations and cultural theories have risen and been summarily abandoned. Is it possible that *The Lore and Language of Schoolchildren* could be written in the same way in the 1990s? And more fundamentally, have today's children created a body of lore and language comparable to that the Opies so sympathetically recorded over forty years ago?

COLLECTING LORE AND LANGUAGE – THE OPIES' LEGACY

Most people have memories of playing games and even recall specific favourite rhymes from their schooldays, but what we know about the generality of children's traditions relies on publications which have transmitted them to a wider audience. Views on how traditions should be recorded in print and which aspects of them were of most significance have changed considerably over time. Specialist collections of 'popular rhymes' current among adults and children first began to appear in the 1840s[3] reflecting Antiquarians' interests in regional history, and material which was old, quaint and unusual. It was not until the 1890s, however, that the results of the first nationwide survey specifically devoted to children's games was published. Alice Bertha Gomme's *Dictionary of British Folklore*, later re-titled *The Traditional Games of England, Scotland and Ireland*[4] was a formidable piece of research which included descriptive analyses of around eight hundred games and their variants from one hundred and twelve locations. It drew on a variety of literary and oral sources, employed the most advanced forms of contemporary methodology and defined children's games as a separate field of study.

Gomme's *Traditional Games* not only set the standard by which later research should be judged, it established a theoretical framework which claimed that games were of special scientific importance. Gomme had seven sons and had noticed that when they and other children were playing, they often imitated adults' actions. She believed that the form of children's play had hardly changed over centuries – perhaps even thousands of years, so she proposed that many games still contained fragments of prehistoric social and religious ceremonies which children had copied from watching adults take part in them. It was therefore quite possible, she concluded, to reconstruct long vanished marriage customs, ancient beliefs involving fire-worship, the rituals of spring festivals and other ceremonials of prehistoric religions by interpreting the dramatic actions and formal choice of circles, lines, spirals or arches which children used in their games. Unknowingly, children at play provided a wealth of information about our ancestors' beliefs that could not be gained from any other source.

Although her work represents the first serious examination of children games, it does have a number of limitations. Gomme's chief focus was on explaining the ancient meaning of traditional activities by relating the form of modern children's games to what she proposed had been done and believed by adults in the past. How children made their games and what they thought about them in the present were of little significance in her study – her theory did not place any emphasis what was popular or enjoyed by children and so she leaves us no evidence of the enthusiasms that kept games alive. Nor was she interested in children's language for its own sake. Gomme carefully recorded all the words which accompanied the dramatic actions of games, making available thousands of examples of Victorian game rhymes which we would otherwise know nothing about. But she maintained that these verses were relatively unimportant aspects of traditional play and, in any case, altered beyond all recognition over fifty or a hundred years of use. Later research has amply demonstrated that rhymes can remain stable over hundreds of years and across wide geographical areas, whilst the forms of games are subject to considerable change. This failure to recognise the persistence of traditional wording is perhaps the most important specific shortcoming of *Traditional Games*. Critically, however, Gomme's theory that children's games owed their existence to ancient customs is also unsupported by historical evidence and based on ideas which have since been disproved. Although it was widely accepted in the nineteenth century, and still appears in popular works even now, there is no scientific basis for suggesting that taboo, tribal marriage customs or fertility rites underlie English customs like morris dancing, mummers plays – or children's games. Today, therefore, *Traditional Games* is most valued for its large number of faithfully recorded games, rather than its theorising.

So monumental was the scholarship and fieldwork on which *Traditional Games* was based, that for over sixty years, few questioned the credibility of Gomme's approach or embarked on substantive new research. Indeed, in an age of film, radio and television, it was widely believed that children barely had any traditions to be collected. Almost all subsequent publications on children's games drew heavily on Gomme's massive collecting, their few examples of new material accompanied by moribund repetition of her outdated theories[5] and dire warnings about the decay of tradition in modern life.

Against such a deadening background, the Opies' decision to involve five thousand children from seventy schools in a survey of rhymes, riddles, jokes, beliefs, 'rites and customs and other curiosities of juvenile lore and language' was as daring as it was innovative. Their approach was determinedly untheoretical – survivals of fertility rituals formed no part of their discussion. Instead they aimed to be as representative of contemporary tradition as possible – the everyday language and customs of ordinary children in 1950s Britain were to be presented in all their untidy reality. The value of the Opies' initiative is readily established and their work achieved wide acclaim, but over the past twenty years, their methodology has also had its critics. Increasingly, the possibility that teachers and publishers acted as 'gatekeepers' of the material children contributed to the study has led to question. Was the language of the rhymes, jokes, riddles and taunts 'cleaned up' or specially selected for publication in *The Lore and Language of Schoolchildren?* Iona Opie has recently highlighted some of the difficulties of the time;

> In our 1950s survey, children did indeed write down vulgar rhymes for us; they knew that the teachers would not look at what they wrote, but would send their contributions straight on to us (that was the agreement). Not that we asked specifically for 'rude' rhymes and jokes; we kept it general, and the 'rude' ones came in along with the other assorted rhymes.

> However, it was editorial policy amongst publishers in the 1950s, not to include dubious material, and that prevented us including anything that was unacceptable to OUP: 'knickers' was the limit. People do not realise how times have changed.[6]

Although there is no guarantee that teachers assisting in the Opies' original survey did not glance through and tactfully remove more vulgar material before it was sent, the sensibilities of both teachers and publishers would surely be less delicate today. Contemporary examples of the Opies' category of 'Parody and Impropriety' like the following could, in all probability, emerge in print unchanged in a *Lore and Language of Schoolchildren 1995:*

> *Good King Wenceslas looked out*
> *Of his bedroom window*
> *Silly bugger he fell out*
> *Landed on a cinder*
> *Brightly shone his bum that night*
> *Though the frost was cruel*
> *When an old man came in sight*
> *Riding on a mule.*[7]

If juvenile vulgarity might be more easily accommodated in the 1990s, however, some subjects featured in children's traditional verse would perhaps raise more questions now than in the 1950s. Would every publisher today want to print a clapping rhyme such as this one collected in Sheffield in 1994?

> *My boyfriend gave me an apple*
> *My boyfriend gave me a pear*
> *My boyfriend gave me a kiss, kiss, kiss* [imitate kissing noise]
> *And threw me down the stairs*
> *He kicked me over London*
> *He kicked me over France*
> *He kicked me over the USA*
> *And I lost my underpants*
>
> *So I gave him back his apples*
> *And I gave him back his pears*
> *And I have him back his kiss, kiss, kiss,* [imitate kissing noise]
> *And I threw him down the stairs*
> *So I kicked him over London*
> *I kicked him over France*
> *I kicked him over Germany*
> *And he lost his underpants.*[8]

The rhyme is a variant of one known throughout the English-speaking world for at least fifty years and also has echoes of the nonsense lines associated with the character of the Doctor in traditional mummers plays and the nursery rhyme 'Goosey, Goosey Gander'. But school reputations are important considerations in a competitive educational market. Potentially, at least, naming a specific institution or area where the rhyme flourished could now be seen as problematic. Despite its respectable antecedents, might it be argued that a school or Education Authority were implicitly condoning assault (with sexual connotations) if they allowed a rhyme such as this to be repeated unchallenged? The little girls who insouciantly chanted it to me were as busy with the accompanying clapping routine as with the meaning of the verses, though they obviously enjoyed the combination of rhyme, metre and words which so expressively warned of precise equality of revenge if boys drew girls into fisticuffs. But would these considerations – which arise from actually seeing the performance – outweigh parental and public concerns about the physical aggression reproduced on the printed page? Overall, in the current climate, publishers might well decide that this particular version of 'My boyfriend gave me an apple' offered too many hostages to fortune and opt for something safer, if less representative of the full range of children's traditions.

Today, potentially controversial material could take many – previously unsuspected – forms. Would every governing body encourage researchers and publishers to associate their school with the irreverence and economy of –

> *Mrs Thatcher*
> *Throw her up and catch her*
> *Squishy, squashy*
> *Squishy, squashy*
> GO TO BED!*[9]* [Spoken in *very* resolute tones]

More seriously, schools working to reduce racism and behaviour that discriminates against children on physical, gender and social grounds, might find a place for classroom discussion of traditional slurs, but not wish to see publications which cited their pupils as sources of songs and rhymes which – even unconsciously – appeared to support discrimination. Taunts like 'specky foureyes' aimed at spectacle wearers since at least the 1830s, skipping rhymes such as 'I Know a Nigger Boy', recorded over at least ten years in the north of England and lowland Scotland but now apparently unknown – or at least unprinted[10] – are hardly cultural treasures. But where such things exist, should they have been collected and when collected should they be published? And although fewer people attend church now, would the sectarian rhymes reproduced in the Opies' frank and evenhanded section on Partisanship, risk causing offence if published in updated form today? Street taunts like 'Catholic cats' and 'Proddy Dogs', 'Get a piece of pork, and stick it on a fork and give it to a Jew boy, Jew' are not edifying – would we risk spreading or re-introducing them by including them in new books? Should respect for others' beliefs preclude open admission of the forms of opposition shown to them in the past – or the present?

As the Opies found in the 1950s, 'rude' rhymes with references to sex and scatology are not uncommon in children's tradition. Usually their expression is saucy or vulgar rather than obscene – but printing rhymes including such content may appear to be giving them official sanction. Should a line still be drawn? And if so, where and by whom? Is it responsible to suggest that everything which might be defined as 'traditional' is a 'valuable part of children's rich oral heritage' and worthy of unqualified support? In 1979, Gershon Legman concluded that far from being complete in its recording of children's linguistic play, *The Lore and Language of Schoolchildren* 'is in fact almost totally expurgated'. Looking at the history of publications on children's lore from the nineteenth century, he proposed that censorship of material by selection of more acceptable variants of rhymes or softening particular words or expressions was the 'ruling case in almost the totality of even the best volumes of this kind.'[11] Despite modifications in attitude to what is acceptable, publishers may continue to feel some rule should be applied – and schools and parents might well agree with them.

But this is not the whole story. Children's traditional culture is an expression of their own beliefs and values, not isolated from contact with the adult world, but specific to themselves. Rhymes and other linguistic play are created and reproduced for children's own purposes, not those of folklorists, the educational system or publishers. Iona and Peter Opie's, *The Singing Game*, a companion to *The Lore and Language of Schoolchildren*, which was published in 1985, amply demonstrates the changing boundaries of public taste. The variants of the clapping game 'When Susie was a Baby' detail its heroine's life from babyhood to beyond the grave and have verses on Susie's teenage years, '... she went "Um, ah, I lost my bra, I left my knickers in my boy friend's car"', as well as descriptions of her work as a stripper – with actions. A hundred years ago, Alice Gomme might have suggested that the game was yet another example of children's tendency to mimic adult behaviour. The Opies noted that the game was extremely popular throughout England, 'little girls of eight or nine being enchanted by the audacity of the words.'[12] It is welcome that today, children's enjoyment of this particular rhyme's bravado can now be indicated through the medium of print, though its content would hardly assure it a place among verses suggested for Junior School study. But acceptability for publication and adult approval are not what this and other aspects of children's thriving, unselfconscious culture are made for. Children create and pass on their rhymes for their own enjoyment as they play. They are a living, active art, made by children for their own purposes, their content to be taken in at children's own level, and that is how they are best understood.

'... THE WAY IT ALL RHYMES' – THE LORE AND LANGUAGE OF TODAY'S CHILDREN

> *Postman Pat, Postman Pat, Postman Pat*
> *Ran over his cat*
> *Blood and guts were flying*
> *Postman Pat was crying*
> *You never saw a flatter cat than that*[13]

No aspect of contemporary culture seems to have been written out of existence more often than children's traditions. In 1892, one of Alice Gomme's correspondents was roundly informed that there was no point in asking for children's games in the area where she lived because they were all 'extinct'[14]. The Opies began their research in the face of warnings that they were starting 'fifty years too late' – children no longer had any folklore. Looking at their three classic volumes of rhymes, beliefs, customs and games today[15], commentators sadly shake their heads and sigh, 'It was all very well for the Opies, they were collecting children's games in the 1950s, when they were still being played. Now children do nothing but watch videos and stare at computer screens. There's no tradition any more.' Such pessimism is no more valid in the 1990s than it was in the 1890s. Children's lore has changed in some respects over the years – it does constantly – but it has certainly not withered under an onslaught of technology led by Sonic the Hedgehog and *Neighbours*. When asked about their traditions in 1994, girls and boys provided convincing evidence of their continuing ability to create new rhymes and adapt old ones. And what's more, to do it just as well as any participants in the Opies' survey in mid-century or Alice Gomme's a hundred years ago.

What supports this tenacious persistence of game rhymes? Children's traditional culture provides a wealth of models and sources which children can draw on to create enjoyable new and adapted verses. Play and games provide a context in which hearing, using and passing on lively rhymes are not merely accepted, but a welcomed aspect of everyday playground life. Creativity and active participation are the norm. But the popularity of rhymes and word play is not just a case of acceptance and habit. The ages at which children are most likely to use game rhymes are also a time when playing with the sound of language is most attractive to them and a stage at which their skills in this area are more developed than their ability to organise other formal qualities of speaking.[16] Sound and rhythm are at least as significant and entertaining as sense, and children's unselfconscious enjoyment or words and sounds for their own sake keeps verses buoyant and alive in the playground's oral tradition. This combination of factors works in similar ways across a range of different circumstances. In 1959, the Opies reported a very widespread rhyme about an unpopular aspect of English lessons –

> *Dictation*
> *Polygation*
> *Three pigs on a railway station.*[17]

At around the same time in Sheffield, the following 'dip' was often used for 'counting out' –

> *Up a ladder, down a ladder*
> *In dictation*
> *How many pussy cats*
> *Went to the station?*
> *Close your eyes and think*
> [child chooses number and 'dipper' counts round, ending]
> *O-U-T spells out!*[18]

The youngest contributor to the examples collected in 1994 is aged 6. She particularly enjoyed a formula used among playmates in the Thames Valley for choosing who is 'on' in games of 'Tiggy'. Her rhyme also provides a clear demonstration of the qualities that underlie tradition's appeal for children –

Ippy dippy dation
My operation
How many nurses
At the station? [19]
[child chooses number and 'dipper' counts last person out]

Rachel's counting out formula makes use of well-established elements of dipping rhymes, like the pairing of the suffix '-ation' and 'station' and the fun of nonsense words which exist for their sound value alone. So although the three rhymes were recorded in different parts of the country, and the collection of Rachel's formula occurred some forty years after the other two, it would be difficult to allocate any to a time or place on the basis of their style and content. They all share an equal measure of delight in language, insistent rhyme and dancing rhythm. Clearly, today's traditions are still being made and recreated in the same ways and for the same reasons as those of the past.

Children are constantly renewing and reworking their existing rhymes – incorporating new fads and topical fashions into well-established formats. Within this process of innovation, however, inclusion in a traditional rhyme often gives an extended life to many real and imaginary characters whose names are faithfully retained in skipping songs and counting out formulae long after they have ceased to be prominent in popular culture. The Opies reported that Lottie Collins, the music hall singer who figured in rather draughty circumstances in the turn of the century rhyme, 'Lottie Collins has no drawers, Will you kindly lend her yours?' had been replaced in the 1950s by the glamourous film star, Diana Dors. As a subject for playground verse, Ms Dors then proved equally durable herself, appearing in a slightly more respectable context in an action rhyme collected in 1986 –

My name is Diana Dors
And I'm a movie star
I've got a cutie, cutie face
And a magic guitar
I've got these legs, legs
Turn around a movie star
A ticker, ticker, ticker, ticker

> *Turn around a movie star*
> *A ticker, ticker, ticker, ticker.*[20]

Most creative changes, however, are more complicated and involve incorporating a variety of new features and functions over time. Combining rhymes used for different purposes, adding a star name and including a brand name, for example, created a series of transformations, in which the beginning of a dipping rhyme collected in the 1950s –

> *I went to a Chinese laundry*
> *To buy a loaf of bread*
> *They wrapped it up in a tablecloth*
> *And this is what they said –*
>   Eenie, meenie, macca, racca, etc.[21]

was changed to reflect a 1980s context, in which restaurants were Chinese and clapping games were the rage –

> *I went to a Chinese restaurant*
> *To buy a loaf of bread, bread, bread*
> *They wrapped it up in a five pound note*
> *And this is what they said, said, said*
> *My name is –*
>   Alli, alli
>   Chickerlye, chickerlye
>   Om pom poodle
>   Walla, walla whiskers
>   Chinese chopsticks
>   Indian chief says 'How!'[22]

In 1994 in Sheffield, the rhyme is still used for a clapping game, but here it features Elvis Presley and its nonsense words have been replaced by an equally imaginative use of standard language –

> *My Nannan sent me shopping*
> *To buy a loaf of bread, bread, bread*
> *She wrapped it up in a five pound note*
> *And this is what she said, said, said*
> *My name is Elvis Presley*
> *Girls are sexy*
> *Sitting in the back room*

> *Drinking Pepsi*
> *Having a baby*
> *In the Royal Navy*
> *Do us a favour –*
> *Get lost.*[23]

It is not necessary for words to change constantly to keep their popularity. 'High, low, dolly, pepper' – a term for fast skipping identical to that given to Gomme – was Katy's response to a request for skipping rhymes in 1994.[24] And when asked for her favourite 'dip', Sarah came up with a formula which, the Opies report, has been delighting children with its 'spell-like jingle' for over a hundred years – sound, rather than sense, underlies its constant form across large areas of northern England and Scotland –

> *Ickle ockle*
> *Chocolate bottle*
> *Ickle ockle out*
> *If you want a chocolate bottle*
> *Please walk out.*[25]

For all the research undertaken on children's rhymes, some aspects of their traditional culture remain entirely mysterious. Why did 'The Tennessee Wig-Walk', Norman Gimbel and Larry Coleman's novelty action song, written in America in 1953 during the short-lived fashion for Rockabilly music, so catch children's imagination that it has turned up in luxuriant variation in playgrounds across Britain ever since?[26] Of the thousands of catchy, musical numbers to come out of Hollywood, what attraction did 'Keep Your Sunny Side Up' exert that caused it to be taken up in the playground and elaborated at different times to incorporate references to Japanese, American GIs, football teams, the glamourous but silent Sabrina (replaced on one Catholic school by Salome), Cliff Richard and even Larry Grayson?[27] And why, among all the chart hits of the 1970s, was KC and the Sunshine Band's, 'That's the Way I Like it', (at number four in the pop charts for ten weeks in 1975) preserved to emerge as an accompaniment to a clapping game in Sheffield in the 1990s –

A-B-C
Let's hit it
That's the way
Ha-ha, ha-ha
I like it
Ha-ha, ha-ha
I like it
Back to back
Front to front
A-B-C
Let's hit it.[28]

In 1971, I began researching game rhymes at a school in a small village in Yorkshire. At the time, it had barely changed since Ralph Vaughan Williams, that archetypal musical evoker of the English country scene, had chosen it as a place to collect folksongs at the turn of the century. The first pupils I met were three little girls from the Reception Class, sitting on a step just next to an old stone stable housing a rather fat pony, who told me their favourite rhyme:

Two white horses
In one stable
Pick one out
And call it Mabel

The verse was used by older children for counting out, but the little girls were too inexperienced in playground games to use it for choosing, they simply enjoyed the metre and the sound of the words. In 1994, Katy, who attends a school in a Derbyshire village, which like most villages now has a central core of old buildings, with infilling and new estates for commuters, told me one of her favourite dips –

My Little Pony
Skinny and bony
Born in a stable
Drinking Black Label

At first sight, the rhyme seems to encapsulate all that has happened in children's physical and cultural environments over the past twenty-odd years – particularly an increasing exposure to commercialism in television adverts and brand names. But, suppose you were to set nostalgia aside and assess the merits of the two dips as cultural products – is the four-square rhythm and literal depiction of the 'White Horses' rhyme really 'superior' to the original imagery and lilting rhythm of 'My Little Pony?' Because of the pioneering work of the Opies, it is possible to demonstrate that children are using change positively. Their research, now stretching over forty-five years, has shown that the processes which children use for creating their rhymes are traditional and operating as securely in the present as in the past. The Opies' legacy allows us to see beyond unsubstantiated generalisations about the wholesale destruction of children's games to recognise the value of their ability to make creative change and give customary shape to innovation.

ACKNOWLEDGMENTS

I am most grateful for the assistance of Katy Coope, Daniel Eades, Joanne Eades, Rachel Garforth, Emma Hallam, Sarah Hallam, Kate Honeyman, Helen Pratt and Rosie Ward Tams who gave time, thought and enthusiasm to the collection of material for this paper and to Iona Opie, whose discussion of the issues surrounding the publication of children's traditions was as generous as it was illuminating.

$\mathscr{R}$EFERENCES

1. Contributed by Emma and Sarah Hallam, Sheffield, South Yorkshire, 1994.
2. Opie, I. and P., (1959) *The Lore and Language of Schoolchildren.* Oxford: Oxford University Press.
3. See for example Chambers, R., (1841) *Popular Rhymes of Scotland,* Edinburgh: W. & R. Chambers, and Orchard Halliwell, J., (1842) *The Nursery Rhymes of England,* London: Frederick Warne & Co. which contain many rhymes still current today.
4. First published in two volumes (1894 and 1898) as the *Dictionary of British Folklore,* London: David Nutt. Later editions, retitled *The Traditional Games of England, Scotland, and Ireland,* have been published (1964) in New York by Dover Publications and most recently (1984) in London by

Thames and Hudson. For more information about this pioneering researcher on children's traditions, see Boyes, G., (1990) 'Alice Bertha Gomme (1852–1938): A Re-assessment of the Work of a Folklorist,' *Folklore*, CI, 2, 198-208.

5. Despite its claims to foreground the art in children's games and game rhymes, a classic late example of this approach is Holbrook, D. (1957) *Children's Games,* Bedford: Gordon Fraser Gallery Limited, whilst ritual explanations which owe a largely unacknowledged debt to Alice Gomme's theories, have made a prominent return in Leyden, M. (1993) *Boys and Girls Come Out to Play: A Collection of Irish Singing Games,* Belfast: Appletree Press Ltd.

6. Iona Opie, Private communication, 18 December 1990. Quoted with permission.

7. Contributed by children from Wickersley, South Yorkshire, 1971.

8. Contributed by Emma and Sarah Hallam, Sheffield, 1994.

9. Contributed by Helen Pratt, Wakefield, West Yorkshire, 1988.

10. G. Boyes Collection, Sheffield, and Richie, J.T.R. (1965) *Golden City,* Edinburgh & London: Oliver & Boyd Ltd, p.132.

11. Legman, G. in *Introduction* to McCosh, S. (1979) *Children's Humour: A Joke for Every Occasion,* St Albans, Herts: Panther Books, p. xv. This extensive study of children's jokes, parodies and rhymes is uncensored and contains much material unprinted elsewhere.

12. Opie, I. and P. (1985) *The Singing Game.* Oxford: Oxford University Press, pp.458–61.

13. Contributed by Katy Coope and Rosie Ward Tams, Holbrook, Derbyshire, 1994. Sung to the 'Postman Pat' signature tune.

14. Letter from Henrietta M. Auden to Alice Gomme, 30 October 1892, Archives of the Folklore Society, University College London. Auden was, she reported, rather amused when only fifteen minutes after this conversation had taken place, she heard a group of little girls playing the singing game 'In and out the windows'.

15. As well as *The Lore and Language of Schoolchildren* and *The Singing Game,* the Opies wrote (1969) *Children's Games in Street and Playground,* Oxford: Oxford University Press.

16. For a more extensive discussion of these aspects of children's language, see Sanchez, M. and Kirshenblatt-Gimblett, B. (1976) 'Children's Traditional Speech Play and Child Language,' in Kirshenblatt-Gimblett, B. (ed.), *Speech Play: Research and Resources for the Study of Linguistic Creativity,* Philadelphia: University of Pennsylvania Press.

17. *The Lore and Language of Schoolchildren,* p.172.

18. G. Boyes Collection, Sheffield.

19. Contributed by Rachel Garforth, Caversham, Bershire, 1994.

20. Contributed by Joanne Eades, Sheffield, 1986. For numerous examples and discussion, see Opie, *The Singing Game,* pp.415–17.

21. Opie, *Children's Games in Street and Playground,* p.41.

22. Opie, *The Singing Game,* p.465.

23. Contributed by Sarah Hallam, Sheffield, 1994.

24. Katy Coope, Holbrook, Derbyshire, 1994. See also *The Traditional Games of England, Scotland, and Ireland,* Vol. II, pp.200–4.

25. Contributed by Sarah Hallam, Sheffield, 1994. Further examples in Opie, *Children's Games in Street and Playground,* pp.32–3.

26. Examples from 1950s to 1980s are printed in Opie, *The Singing Game,* pp.431–3 and held in G. Boyes Collection, recorded in Sheffield 1970.

27. Written by Ray Henderson for the 1929 film 'Sunny Side Up.' See Opie, *The Singing Game,* pp. 429–31 and Boyes, G. (1984), 'Children's Clapping Rhymes from Newfoundland and Sheffield,' *Folk Song Research,* III, 3, 36, referring to versions recorded by the writer in Sheffield 1970 and Newfoundland, Canada 1976, and by Steve Roud in Newcastle-upon-Tyne, Mitcham, Ludgershall and Andover. Roud also notes an Irish version.

28. Contributed by Emma Hallam, Sheffield, 1994. A recording of the song by Dead or Alive also reached number twenty-two in the pop charts in 1984.